USING TABLETS AND APPS
IN LIBRARIES

D1564421

Library Technology Essentials

About the Series

The *Library Technology Essentials* series helps librarians utilize today's hottest new technologies as well as ready themselves for tomorrow's. The series features titles that cover the A–Z of how to leverage the latest and most cutting-edge technologies and trends to deliver new library services.

Today's forward-thinking libraries are responding to changes in information consumption, new technological advancements, and growing user expectations by devising groundbreaking ways to remain relevant in a rapidly changing digital world. This collection of primers guides libraries along the path to innovation through step-by-step instruction. Written by the field's top experts, these handbooks serve as the ultimate gateway to the newest and most promising emerging technology trends. Filled with practical advice and projects for libraries to implement right now, these books inspire readers to start leveraging these new techniques and tools today.

About the Series Editor

Ellyssa Kroski is the Director of Information Technology at the New York Law Institute as well as an award-winning editor and author of 22 books including *Law Librarianship in the Digital Age* for which she won the AALL's 2014 Joseph L. Andrews Legal Literature Award. Her ten-book technology series, The Tech Set, won the ALA's Best Book in Library Literature Award in 2011. She is a librarian, an adjunct faculty member at Pratt Institute, and an international conference speaker. She speaks at several conferences a year, mainly about new tech trends, digital strategy, and libraries.

Titles in the Series

NORTH COUNTRY LIBRARY SYSTEM
Watertown, New York

USING TABLETS AND APPS IN LIBRARIES

Elizabeth Willse

CENTR....... .....RY
WATERTOWN

ROWMAN & LITTLEFIELD
Lanham • Boulder • New York • London

Published by Rowman & Littlefield
A wholly owned subsidiary of The Rowman & Littlefield Publishing Group,
Inc.
4501 Forbes Boulevard, Suite 200, Lanham, Maryland 20706
www.rowman.com

Unit A, Whitacre Mews, 26-34 Stannary Street, London SE11 4AB

Copyright © 2015 by Rowman & Littlefield

All rights reserved. No part of this book may be reproduced in any form or by
any electronic or mechanical means, including information storage and retriev-
al systems, without written permission from the publisher, except by a reviewer
who may quote passages in a review.

British Library Cataloguing in Publication Information Available

Library of Congress Cataloging-in-Publication Data

Willse, Elizabeth, 1978- author.
Using tablets and apps in libraries / Elizabeth Willse.
pages cm. — (Library technology essentials ; 11)
Includes bibliographical references and index.
ISBN 978-1-4422-4389-7 (cloth : alk. paper) — ISBN 978-1-4422-4390-3 (pbk. : alk. paper) —
ISBN 978-1-4422-4391-0 (ebook)
1. Tablet computers—Library applications. 2. Web applications in libraries. I. Title.
Z678.93.T33W55 2015
004.167—dc23
2015019511

∞ ™ The paper used in this publication meets the minimum requirements of
American National Standard for Information Sciences Permanence of Paper
for Printed Library Materials, ANSI/NISO Z39.48-1992.

Printed in the United States of America

This book is dedicated to the information professionals
who helped shape my understanding.

I couldn't have written it without you.

CONTENTS

LIST OF FIGURES AND TABLES

FIGURES

TABLES

SERIES EDITOR'S FOREWORD

The proliferation of tablet devices has brought with it major changes in library programming, services, and resources as libraries strive to accommodate new patron expectations for digital resources such as e-books, apps instruction and support, and even access to the devices themselves. *Using Tablets and Apps in Libraries* is an all-in-one passport to how to develop a successful tablet program in your library. Tablet guru Elizabeth Willse has written an essential guidebook that illustrates how to assess your library's current space, program, and patron needs as well as how to plan, fund, and develop policies for your program. Whether you are hoping to circulate tablets in your library, provide tablet support and training for your patrons (and staff!), use tablets in your storytime programming, or use the devices to promote library services, this is the ultimate field guide.

The idea for the Library Technology Essentials book series came about because there have been many drastic changes in information consumption, new technological advancements, and growing user expectations over the past few years, which forward-thinking libraries are responding to by devising groundbreaking ways to remain relevant in a rapidly changing digital world. I saw a need for a practical set of guidebooks libraries could use to inform themselves about how to stay on the cutting edge by implementing new programs, services, and technologies to match their patrons' expectations.

Libraries today are embracing new and emerging technologies, transforming themselves into community hubs and places of co-creation through makerspaces, developing information commons spaces, and even taking on new roles and formats, all while searching for ways to decrease budget lines, add value, and prove the return on investment of the library. The Library Technology Essentials series is a collection of primers to guide libraries along the path to innovation through step-by-step instruction. Written by the field's top experts, these handbooks are meant to serve as the ultimate gateway to the newest and most promising emerging technology trends. Filled with practical advice and project ideas for libraries to implement right now, these books will hopefully inspire readers to start leveraging these new techniques and tools today.

Each book follows the same format and outline, guiding the reader through the A–Z of how to leverage the latest and most cutting-edge technologies and trends to deliver new library services. The "Projects" chapter comprises the largest portion of the books, providing library initiatives that can be implemented by both beginner and advanced readers accommodating for all audiences and levels of technical expertise. These projects and programs range from the basic "How to Circulate Wearable Technology in Your Library" and "How to Host a FIRST Robotics Team at the Library" to the intermediate, such as "How to Create a Hands-Free Digital Exhibit Showcase with Microsoft Kinect," and to the more advanced options, "Implementing a Scalable E-Resources Management System" and "How to Gamify Library Orientation for Patrons with a Top Down Video Game." Readers of all skill levels will find something of interest in these books.

I have had the pleasure of working with Elizabeth Willse on an online publication project through which I learned that she is not only an outstanding writer but a forward-thinking library professional whose innovate ideas and practical knowledge were sure to make this exceptional book a success. If you have questions about how you can implement a tablet program in your library, this is a book you won't want to miss.

—Ellyssa Kroski
Director of Information Technology
The New York Law Institute
http://www.ellyssakroski.com
http://ccgclibraries.com
ellyssakroski@yahoo.com

PREFACE

Using tablets and apps in your library is a process of making strategic decisions and thinking critically about how different technology options can enhance the programs your library offers and meet your patrons' needs. This guidebook is intended to help you make a strategic plan for using tablets in your library, as well as provide essential tips, tricks, projects, and examples from libraries of different sizes and types.

This is not a guide intended to urge you to buy dozens of tablets for your library and start using them right this minute. Nor is it intended to champion one model of tablet or hardware named in its pages over any other, as the "only right choice" for every library.

Instead, this guide is designed to equip you with questions, processes, and examples to consider as you make decisions about the possibilities of emerging tablet technology. This is a collection of resources to take you from initial planning to the day-to-day workflows of using tablets to provide new services or innovations in the patron services your library already delivers. And of course, learning and working with these tools can build new life into your library programs, and be great fun as well!

ORGANIZATION AND AUDIENCE

This book is designed for libraries and librarians at all stages of the process of using tablets and apps in libraries, whether just beginning to form ideas about choosing devices and apps to creating a brand-new program, or looking for ways to make an existing program run more smoothly.

Chapter 1 will situate your library's proposed device program in the larger context of your patrons' technology use and digital literacy, and help you make the case for starting a device program of your own. Getting Started (chapter 2) takes you through the strategic big picture of what you'll need to do to start a tablet program, from assessing the current state of your library technology and staff, to making proposals and planning purchases, to managing workflows and publicizing your program. Tools and Applications (chapter 3) covers the tools and tasks you'll need to master in order to manage and update your tablets, secure patron data, and keep your device program running, along with guidelines to help you make effective selections of apps for your patrons. Library Examples (chapter 4) will offer profiles of public, academic, and special libraries all over the country already using tablets, and will provide general guidelines that you can adapt to your own tablet program, no matter its focus or size. Library Projects (chapter 5) will guide you through a few sample projects to start using tablets in your library. Tips and Tricks (chapter 6) is a quick-reference section full of tips that will help with the nitty-gritty details of getting your program launched and keeping it going. Future Trends (chapter 7) discusses some of the innovations the future of tablets might hold, and some of the ways that librarians can prepare. Recommended Reading is a collection of books, web resources, white papers, presentations, conferences, and blogs recommended for ongoing learning.

ACKNOWLEDGMENTS

Thank you to my parents and my family, born and chosen, for their love and support and encouraging my librarian dreams. Thank you to Brian, Chris and Rachel, Evans, Maegan, Russ, and the Squirrels. Thank you, Jean Hines, Barbara Genco, Ellyssa Kroski, Irene Lopatovska, Lisa Peet, Peter Otis, Pamela Outwin, Sam Howard, and all the Pratt Institute School of Information and Library Science (SILS) professors and students who taught and mentored me in and out of the classroom. Thank you to Erika Spelman, who bridges the gaps. Thank you to the generous community of librarians from Metropolitan New York Library Council (METRO), Special Libraries Association (SLA), American Libraries Association (ALA), and on social media who encouraged me and helped me find resources. Enormous thanks to all who advised and contributed their experience and knowledge, as well as sharing their own library stories: Cheryl Abdullah-Abouelaziz, Scott Bonner, Rachel Nicole Capdarest-Arest, Rachel Castro, Farrukh Farid, Trevor Hanel, Jeff Jarvis, Annmarie Hurtado, Jennifer Driscoll, and Deborah Takahashi, Michelle Kraft, Jared Leadbetter and Kate Pickup-McMullin (and the ninjas!), Liz Connell and Claire Moore, David Lee King, Gretchen King, Michelle Kraft, Mark Mautone, Alisha Miles, Stan Pollakoff, Lee Rainie, Laura Rifkin, Bonnie Roalsen, Isa Small and Laura Miller, Jennifer Hubert-Swan, Sally-Adrina Taylor, Stacy Taylor, Kelvin Watson, Abbie Weinberg and David Woodbury. Last, thank you to the team at Rowman and Littlefield, especially Assistant Editor Darren Williams, who was wonderful to work with throughout the process.

I

AN INTRODUCTION TO TABLETS AND APPS

As you may have already seen in your library, the ownership of tablet and mobile devices is on the rise. As of 2014, over half of American adults own some form of handheld device, whether a reader or a tablet (Zickuhr and Rainie 2014). Portable, powerful touch screen-powered tablet computers are becoming key parts of your library patrons' information landscape and everyday life, influencing the way patrons connect with work and family, the way they seek and consume information for education or pleasure, and the way they manage all facets of daily life from office to health resources to recipes for dinner.

Consumers using tablets are able to choose between a variety of sizes, capabilities, and operating systems, and to populate their chosen devices with apps and accessories that help them seek information, stay connected, and have fun. Since the introduction of the first iPad in 2010 (Steele 2013), Apple's tablets and their operating system have dominated the tablet marketplace (IDC Worldwide 2015). Other tablets that have entered the marketplace include the Google Nexus (powered by Android OS), the Kindle Fire, and the Microsoft Surface tablet. With larger screens, better processing speeds, and versatile ranges of apps, some cell phone models, known as "phablets," are blurring the lines between cell phone and tablet computer as our constantly connected, bring your own device (BYOD) culture is on the rise.

Rising, also, is the number of patrons who seek help in getting the most out of their devices, especially at peak times for new device acquisition, back to school and holiday gift-giving (IDC Worldwide 2014). They value the ability to turn to libraries for this kind of education and support. As seen in the Pew Research Center's Typology of American Library Users, enthusiastic proponents of library use span socioeconomic, age, and geographic barriers, as well as levels of technological expertise, but are unified by the value they place on the library as a community resource (Zickuhr, Purcell, and Rainie 2014). It's worth noting that the enthusiasm for the library transcending levels of income and digital literacy was reported in 2013, just one year after the first iPad tablet became commercially available. Library patrons are curious and engaged with the devices they have in hand, or with plans to access and learn about the ones they have not yet purchased. Libraries have long been resources to support exploration and education as well as providing access to resources as equalizers to answer information needs and bridge the digital divide. To help maintain a responsive position as an information resource, and nurture patrons' enthusiasm, it makes sense for librarians to stay educated about the broad landscape of devices, apps, and platforms, both those in place in our library and in the larger context.

In an increasingly and constantly connected world, digital access and critical digital literacy have become embedded in all aspects of everyday life. Access to technology and developing technological skills have become essential to even the most basic tasks of completing an education, staying connected with friends and loved ones, seeking a job, participating in civic decisions, filing taxes, or managing personal health information. Navigating the constant flow of information means having access and learning new skills of finding, evaluating, sorting, and responding to information by producing new knowledge (Aspen Institute 2014).

With the ability to offer patrons access to digital resources both in and out of the library, the role of the library, and the librarian as mentor and curator, has become increasingly important, even as it shifts to accommodate the faster flow and wider availability of information resources and the changes in patrons' information-seeking behavior. While the information offered is no longer bound by its physical borders, the library as a physical space is still an important community resource, offering patrons a welcoming "third place" (Annoyed Librarian 2014), cutting across the confines of family, school, or work to invite learning and an exchange of ideas. To help patrons stay connected and develop a critical set of digital literacy skills, libraries and librarians need to learn, and to build, programs that harness the power of the emerging tablet technology to invite both judicious consumption of information and the skills to make new information.

Working with patrons in the connected mobile landscape means changing the way we, as librarians, manage and think about our libraries. Entirely bookless libraries, such as BiblioTech in Bexar, Texas (McFarland 2014) or the school library at Florida Polytechnic University (Flood 2014), have built their resources and programs entirely around digital offerings. It can mean acquiring new devices, training staff, and launching brand-new programs, such as app demonstrations, coding classes, or playful tinkering with brand-new app-driven devices in makerspaces.

But it doesn't have to mean a change that drastic for your professional practice and your library.

When you and your library choose to bring the potential of tablets and apps into your library, you and your patrons will be learning and adapting to new options and new workflows. But you will also, and most important, be building on services the library has always provided and skills you have always brought to the library profession. As you will discover in these pages, many of the knowledge bases you'll draw on to make your tablet program a success are already in place in the departments of your library—IT and technological expertise, collection development and evaluation, managing circulation and access services, guiding patrons, and promoting library services with outreach. No matter how cutting edge or exciting the technology (and it truly is!), this book will take you back to basics.

Hopefully, reading this far has gotten you excited to launch your own tablet program. Researching and drafting a proposal are covered more extensively in the next chapter. For now, here's a brief guide to how to make a case for a tablet program.

MAKING A CASE FOR A TABLET PROGRAM ... AND KNOWING WHEN NOT TO

- **Arm Yourself with Data:** Draw on electronic circulation statistics and mobile access of the site, and build in larger population data about device use from reputable sources. Remember those statistics about increasing device use and library enthusiasm from both the digitally savvy and digital novice learners.

- **Relate Your Tablet Program to Your Library's Goals**: Be ready with a specific answer to the question: "How will investing in a tablet program uniquely support our library's goals and serve our patrons?" (Key answers will involve access, learning resources, and teaching digital skills, regardless of your library size.)
- **Focus on What's Already in Place**: Make a case emphasizing what you already have: subscription resources, IT expertise, operations workflows, storage space, staff knowledge, technology that can be adapted and repurposed, partnerships for grants, and patrons willing to donate time or expertise.
- **Present a Budget Emphasizing Comparison and Function**: For every device, hardware, or software purchase you advise, present price comparisons that highlight that you've found the best, most reliable "bang for your buck," especially if you're championing cutting-edge technology over an older or more middle-of-the-road model.
- **Anticipate Objections:** Anticipating objections to your proposed tablet program and preparing sound counterarguments helps strengthen the case for a program. Present a clear plan for how training for and running a program will fit into existing workflows to counter the objection that the program will strain staff schedules. To counter the argument that lack of device use among patrons indicates a lack of interest in the program, emphasize the necessity of developing new digital literacy skills. With a little forethought, many anticipated objections can be turned around into a reason to support the program.
- **Know When Not to Launch the Program:** However, there are some cases where your library may not be ready to launch its own device program . . . just yet. In some cases, especially if it is clear that the staff and technology infrastructures are not in place to support the program, or if the proposed tablet uses conflict with your library's established technology platforms and systems, it may be wise to wait, and use the time to research and refine the plan.

Armed with critical skills in information literacy to evaluate new technologies and electronic resources, librarians, especially those affiliated with larger academic institutions or corporations, can be invaluable resources to technology initiatives in the larger community as well. Librarians' familiarity with the information and interfaces of topical electronic resources, experience in conducting library instruction, and working with privacy issues and technology and information use policies makes them a great asset to have for any team launching a tablet program. Learning about different options for tablet use equips librarians to advise other departments or patrons about the decisions they need to make and the tools they need to assemble in order to launch a device program. That expertise also positions them to caution against a too-hasty adoption of a program. "The adoption of any technology depends heavily on whether an institution has the infrastructure to support it" (Kraft 2013a). If taking the time to work through the logistics and costs to support a tablet program's goals has taught you that it's not the right time, you don't have to start right now. Taking extra time to learn what other libraries are doing, and what's available, will only make your program better when you do start. Even if your library has postponed or decided against working with tablets for now, learning about tools, apps, tips, and tricks will help you assist patrons who come to you for advice.

This is a guide to help you, as a librarian, use tablets effectively to do what you've always done: think critically, ask the right questions, build digital literacy, and deliver the resources and programs that help your patrons do the same.

Ready to get started? Turn the page.

2

GETTING STARTED WITH TABLETS AND APPS

Maybe it begins with a children's librarian coming back to the branch from ALA full of ideas and enthusiasm, presenting a plan to the trustees. Perhaps it begins when a citywide library system seizes the opportunity of a grant. It could be the realization of a farseeing budget decision accounted for three years ago, or part of collaboration with schools or other organizations, a donation, or part of a statewide technology initiative.

A successful tablet program can begin from any one of a number of entry points, whether it is intended for one device, five, fifteen, or fifty. No matter how it begins, launching a tablet program in your library or library system requires much of the same kind of planning as any other new project. It needs assessment of a few key factors: community needs, staff training, and available resources. Whether it is a formal document or part of a presentation before your supervisor or the board, a strong proposal should include building the tablet program's goals into the library's overall strategy, as well as outlining plans for factors like budget and a realistic timeline to roll out the program. Working through a few initial assessments and figuring out answers to a few logistical questions will help make for a successful program.

Before you begin the program, you will need to work through planning the logistics of operating the program and crafting policies and procedures to document rules and procedures. You will want to pull together an understanding of your current available resources and patron needs to present them in the larger context of the goals of your library system and the community. Knowing where you stand will help you know where, and how, you need to draw on additional research. Whether you're using these planning documents to get board or administrative approval before implementing the program, or whether you're at the level to go ahead on your own initiative, making sure the logistics work on paper is a key first step.

ASSESSING CURRENT TECHNOLOGY RESOURCES

Knowing where your current technology resources stand allows you to decide how to integrate your new tablet program into existing technology, or shape proposed plans to the systems already in place, at the branch library level or that of the larger library system. You will want to consider any operating systems currently used to keep library systems running smoothly, to ensure compatibility of new devices. You will also want to consider the existing systems in place to deliver Internet and Wi-Fi to your staff and patrons, to make sure that the proposed device program will not slow down the bandwidth shared by staff and patrons using desktops and devices at the library's busiest times.

Whether you choose to dedicate one of your existing computers to be the master computer for the tablet program at this stage, or budget funds to purchase a new computer, will depend on an assessment of the age and functionality of the current computer system and how the plan for upgrades, updates, and other technical support currently functions. Because the length of time needed for charging and updating devices can be unpredictable, and can often take longer than anticipated, you will want to consider setting up a dedicated desktop to use as the tablet maintenance station. If tablets are part of a patron-facing program, particularly lending, you need to make sure you budget adequate time and computer resources for resetting borrowed tablets back to their default settings to preserve patron privacy, as well as to allow for charging or for software updates. For example, it can take four to five solid hours to fully charge an iPad that has completely drained its battery (and many devices will be returned in this state). Also, remember that things like software updates, whether system-wide or manual, can often take longer than anticipated, especially under the existing Wi-Fi and bandwidth demands of a busy library.

Don't forget to consider things like electricity and outlet placements in the planning stages for the location of your library's new tablet program. As you consider choosing a space in the library to be the program's home base, make sure there are adequate outlets, or surge-protected power strips in place and ready to hand. Extra outlets are always appreciated. If the proposed tablet program would require rearranging the current technology layout substantially, or adding a significant number of iPads, docking stations, or the addition of more than one or two desktop computers to the library's existing system, you may want to discuss the plans with building or facilities management.

In assessing whether the current technology can meet program needs, the following questions can be helpful.

QUESTIONS TO ASSESS CURRENT TECHNOLOGY

- What existing hardware can the library use to help launch the program and what will need to be purchased to get a tablet program up and running?
- What device and software requirements are tied to your existing vendor relationships? (While most programs and apps are designed to work across numerous platforms, there can be exceptions or glitches.)
- What partnerships and resources could help this program run more smoothly? Whether drawing on financial or operational resources from the larger library system or the teaching skills of enthusiastic professors in different departments, or arranging demonstrations from tech-savvy entrepreneurs based in the community, reaching out can make launching a program easier. Depending on your particular library's situation, you may also be able to reach out for donations of devices, hardware, or financial resources.
- How will the timeline for the project account for testing new technology and remedying any glitches that may arise?

Working through the logistics of the areas outlined above will help strengthen your action plan, as well as give you better answers to key questions to get any necessary buy-in or secure partnerships or funding.

ASSESSING STAFF RESOURCES IN YOUR ORGANIZATION

When planning a tablet program, knowing what resources are available to you at every organizational level, as well as potential partnerships, can help form the action plan.

Questions to Assess Staff Readiness

Make sure you are ready to answer the following questions about resources and responsibilities for launching the program.

- Who will need to approve funding and workflows for the program? Will the decision be made at the individual branch or department level, or does it need to move through at the board or statewide level first?
- What will the program's staffing needs be? You will need to ensure staff responsibility and hours for

    1. Planning and managing the program.
    2. Selecting and purchasing equipment and apps.
    3. Initial setup of the devices, including adequate time to test proposed apps and in-house programs.
    4. Training existing staff in areas like device operation, app selection, and program development.
    5. Outreach and education for patrons to show the tablets' and program's potential and build a user base. This includes planning, scheduling, and running the program in different departments and branches.
    6. Upkeep and troubleshooting for the devices and their platforms: an unpredictable, time-consuming, but necessary task. Will maintaining the system and devices involve partnership with IT staff or departments at your branch, or offsite?

- What level of comfort and training does the current staff have with different devices and apps? Their existing skill sets can play a role in deciding to develop a program based on apps and ideas your staff already embraces. Alternately, assessing your staff's current skill sets might indicate the need for training, such as setting up a Technology Petting Zoo (see chapter 5).

PATRON ASSESSMENTS

As you begin to plan the goals and audience for your iPad program, you will need to know more about your patron population's current device preferences, as well as any unmet needs for technology or learning that could help drive attendance to your program.

Your library may already be collecting useful data to lay the groundwork for a tablet needs assessment. Demographic data about your patron community gathered to help draft effective collection development policies can help inform your assessment for a tablet program. So can circulation statistics showing an increase in digital downloads, or website statistics reflecting increased hits or access of the library's site through the mobile app. Learning about your patrons' device use could be as simple as observation. When you start to see more patrons consulting iPads or tablets as they ask reference questions or browse the stacks, it's a good assumption that programs exploring the potential of tablets and apps will be well received.

Survey questions and focus groups provide more targeted approaches to gathering data about patron preferences for tablet and app uses. Because these approaches place demands on patrons' time more directly, surveys and focus groups are best used to address a specific question about patron needs, or the value of library programs, such as assessing the way a specific patron population (for example, a particular age group) already uses technology, or what they think about existing or potential library programs. Depending on the demographics of your patron base, you may want to make time for multiple focus groups or surveys, to tailor both the questions and the data collection to the interests and technology experience of your existing library patrons.

Free, web-based forms like SurveyMonkey and Google Forms are available to help collect data about patrons' current device use and interest in potential programs. A web-based survey can be distributed on the library's website and through social media. Because you can design survey questions as multiple choice (pick one, or check off a selection that applies), online survey questions are good for gathering and analyzing specific answers in detail, such as learning about patrons' existing technology practices or feelings about a specific range of programs. For an online survey, you will want to limit your questions to no more than ten or fifteen questions focusing on a specific area or aspect of your program.

While it does require a significant investment of planning at the outset, running a focus group can be a rich source of candid information from patrons. It is best to use a focus group to discuss a specific issue such as how patrons currently perceive and use library technology, what their frustrations with it have been, and what they would like to see the library develop in the near future. It's important to remember that the information gained in a focus group will be subjective, and can vary, depending on the group dynamic. Your facilitator will need to be prepared to steer the discussion, both in terms of the topics and in drawing out some more reticent participants while making more talkative group members feel valued.

Setting up a focus group to assess current patron needs or thoughts about a proposed tablet program requires a significant amount of planning, in terms of structuring the topics and the kinds of questions that will be asked, and planning for the time and logistics (such as recruitment, facilitation, and analysis of the responses) involved. You will want to recruit (and confirm, and remind) a selection of about seven to ten members of your target group, with the understanding that recruitment does not necessarily guarantee their attendance at the date and time of the group. Rather than have just one staffer running the group, you will want to have one to lead actively and a second to record the proceedings, either digitally or by taking notes. From start to finish, it is wise to budget approximately two hours for the group itself. You will want to begin with a prepared explanation introducing the topic of the focus group and the questions it seeks to answer, about current technology use, for example, or about ways the library can improve or develop new tablet programs. You will want to introduce the idea of the focus group itself: a group exchanging ideas and respecting each other's opinions in conversation. You will also want to ask their permission to record their responses.

Plan to ask four or five questions over the course of the focus group. The process of crafting specific questions for your focus group will vary based on your library or department's population and needs, but here are some ideas to help you get started. See the resources section for more ideas.

1. What devices do you currently use to access library services?
2. What programs do you wish the library would run?
3. What library services do you access on your device most often?
4. What are the most useful features about the library website (or app)?
5. Tell us a story about a frustration you encountered with the library's apps.

As you can see from the sample questions above, focus groups can be effective to help propose and plan for new technology projects, as well as to monitor a program's success and assess whether the programs you are running are meeting their proposed goals as well as meeting patrons' needs.

Working with the information gathered in the focus group can be time-consuming, in terms of transcribing and analyzing the data. You will want to see what patterns and themes emerge, where emotions like enthusiasm and frustration run high, and what desires for new services are expressed. Looking at the big picture of focus group responses will help you create a basis of patron-driven data to support the structure and goals of your proposed tablet program.

DEVELOPING YOUR PLAN WITH RESEARCH

In addition to assessing the available resources and patron needs, you will want to pull in research that situates your goals for a tablet program in a larger context. As you know from the other reports that are part of your library life, pulling together the right supporting numbers can strengthen your proposed plan. The following resources can also be helpful in making a case for the tablet program (see chapter 1):

- The Pew Research Center is a terrific source of reports on technology use, social media, and libraries (http://www.pewinternet.org/).
- ALA's Office of Research and Statistics provides a number of useful Issues Briefs specifically to help librarians pull together reports (http://www.ala.org/offices/ors). The Digital Inclusion Survey published with research partners at University of Maryland can be especially useful to public libraries advocating for technology in their communities, (http://digitalinclusion.umd.edu/).
- For programs focused on children, take a look at reports from the Fred Rogers Center for Early Learning and Children's Media at St. Vincent's College (http://www.fredrogerscenter.org/resources/publications/), or The Joan Ganz Cooney Center at Sesame Workshop (http://www.joanganzcooneycenter.org/).

CREATING EFFECTIVE POLICIES FOR A TABLET PROGRAM

There are two aspects of ensuring sound policy for your tablet program. First, you will need to make sure that the proposed uses for your tablets adhere to the overarching policies governing your library's digital resources, collection development, copyright, materials, and funding allocations. Second, you will want to make sure that the rules and procedures outlining how tablets will be used in library programs or accessed by patrons are clearly outlined. You will want to build planning time to coordinate policies and procedures across departments, particularly IT and technology committees, digital resource managers, catalogers, and the staffer in charge of managing any licenses and rights for your systems. Taking the time for this level of coordinated communication will be helpful in drafting the policy as well as making sure to have clear communication about shared staff responsibilities and workflows.

Make sure to draft and get any necessary approvals for policies to cover acquisition and maintenance of any new devices, as well as policies to guide how they will be used, whether onsite or as part of a lending program. If the new devices are going to be checked out to patrons, either for in-library or home use, make sure to document the guidelines and policies for routine lending, as well as for resetting the iPads in between patron uses to protect patron privacy. Pull together and use key language and guidance from your library's existing policies on materials selection, patron access privileges, and rules and procedures for borrowing and assessing fines for overdue/damaged materials to build a framework.

Some areas of policy you will want to address especially closely in policy and procedural documentation are

- Policies for evaluating, selecting, and budgeting for new devices, software, and equipment.
- How any devices used will be backed up, including account information, timing of routine backups, and plans for wiping patron information or other sensitive data between uses.
- Protections against damage of the devices, peripherals, or operating systems, as well as assigning specific fees or penalties to be charged in the event of damage.
- How device use and peripherals will be cataloged, and how usage statistics will be tracked.
- Copyright and digital licensing issues that may arise in the use or purchase of new digital resources.
- How the metrics of the success of the program will be evaluated.
- Staff and departmental responsibilities for the devices, including ways their use will be scheduled and shared between departments, responsibility for necessary troubleshooting and maintenance, and even who will charge and back up the devices.
- Collection development policies to help curate the apps and programs on tablets. (There will be more on apps in the next chapter.)

ASSESSING CURRENT SPACE AND PROGRAM SPACE NEEDS

The amount of space needed for launching your tablet program will depend, of course, on the nature of the program being planned, the number of tablets being purchased, and the ways patrons and staff will be using the tablets as part of library programs in-house or offsite. For example, in order to incorporate tablets as part of a librarian-led presentation or activity, you may be able to use an existing library space. You might turn the space already allotted for children's story hour into a site for enhanced, tablet-driven story hours or an app presentation space by adding a projection screen. To do so, you will need to plan for the way additional equipment takes up the space, or projection or tablet screens change your audience's sight lines.

If the tablets are intended to be part of collaborative activity, how many users will be working with the views and touch screens of a single tablet? In addition to making sure to have adequate table space and seating at accessible levels for each group using a tablet, you will want to make sure that the lighting in your space minimizes glare on the tablets' glass screens during their use. Because different apps and Wi-Fi can drain tablets in often unpredictable ways, you may want to ensure that your program setup for patron use allow for charging during use. Another solution would be to purchase more tablets than you anticipate being used concurrently in one program so that some of them can be charging between programs.

Tablets that are intended for in-house patron or staff use will need to be mounted on some kind of stand. Depending on the available space and layout of your library, options include wall-mounted, fixed onto a table, or freestanding on the floor. (If using a freestanding option, make sure it is weighted or secured to the floor.) Plan to secure tablets intended for patron use to the stands, both as a deterrent against theft and to minimize wear and tear. Some stands come equipped with security features as part of their hardware. Alternately, locking mechanisms can be purchased separately. Something as simple as a plastic zip-tie can even be used as a cheap, if not fantastically secure, solution.

Storage for Tablets

Whether using tablets as part of a loaner program, mounting them on stands in the library, or bringing them out for specific patron programs, you will need to plan for secure storage and charging space for the tablets. Using existing storage closets or cabinets might be secure, but may not allow for charging, which would mean setting aside additional time and space to charge the devices after they have returned from borrowing or programs.

There are a number of commercially available storage carts that can secure tablets when not in use. Different vendors and catalogs will use different terms, like "iPad storage carts," "tablet carts," "Chromebook carts," and "laptop storage" carts to describe items with similar features, so you will want to use combinations of those terms to research the capacity, dimensions, prices, and other features of different carts to find what meets your program's needs. Carts can be purchased from library and school furniture vendors, as well as from office supply and technology stores. Prices, size, storage capacity, and customer support will vary between different models and vendors of carts. It may be that your existing vendor relationships with library furniture suppliers or office suppliers will determine your selection of stands and storage carts. If making the selection of storage carts on behalf of your library, or at your own purchasing discretion, you will want to do any hands-on research you can manage at trade shows, other libraries, as well as area schools and colleges or small businesses.

You will want to plan for and shop for storage options after you have some idea of the model and dimensions of the tablets you are planning to purchase for your program. You will also want a rough idea of the number of devices being purchased (both initially and for future expansion of the program). Some tablet storage carts can accommodate devices and models of different dimensions and could be used to store tablets of different models as well as laptops in one cart unit. Others come with adjustable shelving. Some carts have the capacity to charge tablets while storing them securely under lock and key. If your plans for programming include moving multiple tablets between areas or departments of your library, you will want to make sure to select a wheeled cart. If you decide to purchase a storage cart, you may want to purchase one with the capacity for additional tablets beyond your initial pilot program purchase, to allow for growth.

Accessories for Tablets

In addition to planning for storage, security, and stands for your tablets' use, you will want to plan for additional replacements for small peripheral accessories that will see a lot of wear and tear. Make sure that any loaner tablet is outfitted with a carrying case that can hold charging cords, sync cords, and a pair of headphones. Plan to invest in durable protective cases for tablets that are going to see a lot of hands-on use from younger patrons especially. As part of both your program's initial budget, and its ongoing maintenance, plan to purchase multiple spares of any small accessories. For every tablet in your program, make sure to budget for at least two or three extra charging cords, USB syncing cables, and sets of headphones. Speaking of important small items, remember to budget for ongoing purchases of disinfectant wipes and screen cleaners, and to make wiping the physical devices clean just as much a part of routine maintenance as wiping their digital data!

BUDGETING AND SEEKING FUNDING FOR THE TABLET PROGRAM

The funding and financing of your tablet program will involve significant initial expenses, such as the purchases of devices, accessories, software, hardware such as docking or mounting stations, storage space, and any licenses needed for the new devices. Make sure to budget for the ongoing care of the tablets as well, to account for wear and tear on physical systems and supporting hardware, as well as any needed software upgrades. Depending on the way your library structures its technology and operations budgets, you may be able to draw on funds earmarked for your library's technology projects.

In some cases, the process of securing and managing funding for a new tablet program will be nearly identical to your library's process of seeking funding for other materials and initiatives. Depending on your proposed program's place in the larger library infrastructure, you may need to appeal to a central branch, state library organization, board of trustees, or town budget committee. Collaboration with other branches or library systems to share resources or secure joint funding may be an effective strategy.

Grants can be an effective source of funding to launch a new technology project. Grants geared toward technology and educational development, for libraries, nonprofits, and other educational institutions, can be a great resource. Regionally specific grants may be available at the state and local level as well.

Getting Started with Grants

The following is a partial list of organizations that can be good resources for grants to help start your tablet program.

- **Grants.gov** (http://www.grants.gov/). This is a searchable central website to help find federally funded grant opportunities.
- **Institute of Museum and Library Services** (http://www.imls. gov/). In addition to administering the Libraries Services and Technology Act, the IMLS maintains a searchable list of available grants seeking applicants. While the "Libraries" and "Archives" categories are likely the best sources, browse other categories that may also suit your institution's needs.
- **Loleta D. Fyan Grant** (http://www.ala.org/offices/ors/orsawards/ fyanloletad/fyanloletad). Administered by ALA, this grant is intended to support programs that improve libraries and their services with innovations that are responsive to the library's future needs.

Sometimes an unanticipated windfall can be the source of the funding that launches your program. In October of 2012, Hurricane Sandy caused catastrophic damage to communities in Brooklyn and Queens, New York, including libraries and their collections. In 2013, Google worked with the State of New York to donate Nexus tablets to both the Brooklyn and Queens library systems (Epps and Watson 2014). This donation allowed each library to build in-house programs and a tablet lending program around Google's tablet technology.

FACTORS TO CONSIDER IN TECHNOLOGY PURCHASES

Getting your tablet program started will mean choosing between devices and operating systems. Factors like compatibility with your current technology and your patrons' reported preferences and needs will play a role in the choice of operating systems. Building a program around multiple devices and platforms is also an option, but only if your library has sufficient patron interest, staff training, IT and infrastructure support, and budget resources to launch a program incorporating multiple devices. Even with all of those resources readily available, it may be more manageable to plan, test, and launch one device platform at a time, to build your multiplatform tablet program more methodically. Once you've made the choice of Android tablets, iPads, or Microsoft Surface tablets, your decision-making is far from over. You will need to select the size and models for the types of devices you plan to use, as well as selecting hardware like carrels for storage and display or mounting stations for patron access. You will need to purchase some means of securing any devices intended for in-library patron use. This can either be a specialized locking mechanism, or something as simple as a set of zip-ties. You will also need to be prepared to purchase extras of some of the peripherals, like power cords, to account for wear and tear, or loss of the smaller items.

Gathering information and reviews from sources such as *Consumer Reports* and *TechCrunch,* as well as from library-related sources like *Library Journal,* InfoDOCKET, ACRL, LITA, and your own professional network is a good first step to familiarize yourself with the technology you're thinking of adopting. However, there is no substitute for spending some time hands-on with the same model of tablet or version of app you're considering implementing in your library. Whether that means visiting a local academic library with a program already in place, borrowing a device from a friend or colleague, or even spending some time at the Apple Store or BestBuy trying out different device options, plan to put in time to explore both the capabilities and overall feel of the device and programs you are considering purchasing. Vendors at professional conferences can offer hands-on time as well. In addition to any library-related conferences you attend, be on the lookout for tech-related conferences or expos in your area. If choosing tech is a key part of your responsibility for a proposed project, you may be able to get management to help defray the cost of a pass to a conference that lets you get a better feel for the devices.

While doing your own research and hands-on experience are important ways to develop an understanding of the feel and features of the different tablet, software, and accessory options, a partnership with your IT departments, at the branch and system-wide level is, ultimately, even more important to getting your tablet program started. Plan to coordinate with your IT department immediately after the program begins to take shape, and periodically throughout the planning, ordering, setup, and pilot phases of the program. Not only will they provide ongoing support to keep the tablets running smoothly, but they will be able to provide the information about the features of different devices and systems and their compatibility with existing library systems. In some library systems, the IT department is solely responsible for making the decisions about purchasing new technology. Based on an understanding of the programs and audiences proposed for the tablet program in your library, the IT department may determine the operating system, size and model of tablets, and accessories to be purchased, as well as sourcing and pricing them from vendors and handling budgeting.

Even if the final purchasing decision for devices, operating systems, and accessories is out of your hands, research and experience with the resources above—along with working through the other phases of planning your tablet program's technology, staffing needs, and audience—will help you communicate more clearly with your IT department about your proposed program's technology needs and development.

PUBLICITY FOR YOUR TABLET PROGRAM

Once the tablets and equipment for your program have been ordered and tested, and the program is starting to take more tangible shape, it is a good time to begin building interest with outreach. Ideally, connect with and get tips from colleagues working in public services and outreach to coordinate promotion for the tablet program. They can use the library's existing structure of announcements, through newsletters or social media, to drum up interest in the features of the tablet program. Publicity for the program could be as simple as scheduling a few tweets or blog posts, or adding engaging signage near the areas where tablets will be used or available for checkout. Especially if your tablet program is the pilot for your library system or region, you may want to draft a press release to share with local print and online media.

Turning the launch of the program into a celebration for a few hours on an afternoon is a way to generate patron interest. However, if you go that route, be mindful of a few potential logistical hurdles. If you plan to showcase the launch of the program as an event, you will have to budget for staff time to prepare and publicize the event itself, as well as organizing and budgeting for things like snacks. Also, as many librarians involved in live tablet programming can attest, be prepared to react to and work around any technological glitches that will, inevitably, happen while a roomful of patrons are watching intently.

Some of the publicity for your tablet program will come from the ongoing program itself. If tablets are mounted in the library for patrons to access freely, make sure that the majority of your staff are trained to demonstrate the basic functions and do some troubleshooting so that they are prepared to help patrons on the fly as needed. Presenting tablets' interactive capabilities in activities like multimedia storytimes for patrons, or to teach about the tablets and apps themselves, will help spur patron interest. Having librarians guide patrons through programs using tablets and apps helps publicize the program, as well as teaches them skills and digital literacy.

THE ACTION PLAN AND PROPOSAL

Working through the decisions and logistics outlined thus far should put you on comfortable footing to create a proposal or presentation to begin using tablets in your library.

Briefly Describe the Program's Objective and Logistics. Will the tablets be used for live programming, patron borrowing, or mounted as permanent features in the library? (You may want to write this part of the proposal last, as an executive summary.)

Provide Context for the Program Using Data. Pull together key themes and justifications situating patron assessment data in the larger context of your library's strategy and overarching technology statistics and trends.

Include Graphics and Screenshots. Show the tablets being used (or a projection of a live demonstration if you're presenting your ideas in person).

Describe How the Program Will Be Administered. Include the role of the IT department and a brief timeline of staff training, as well as policy.

Present a Budget Including Devices, Hardware, Software Licenses, and Peripherals. Include plans to solicit donations and grants.

Document Your Timeline. Outline the time from assessment through research through setup, training, and a soft launch demonstrating the program to staff, to rehearsal before the full launch. Allow extra time for training, testing, and troubleshooting. (Allow at least an extra week at every phase, if possible.)

Start Small. Plan a pilot program for a particular department, branch, or demographic, working with a small number of devices.

Describe Publicity Plans. Briefly outline the ways you will reach the program's target audience.

Describe Metrics for Success. How and when will the program's goals be assessed? What numbers will evaluate the program's success? What will indicate readiness for the transition from pilot to a wider launch?

Plan for Troubleshooting. Present a brief outline of potential pitfalls and account for staff responsibilities and potential fixes.

With these basic ingredients and a few eye-catching graphics, you're ready to present your proposed program to your manager, your library board, or even potential funders to help get it launched. With a few tweaks, you can adapt parts of the proposal above to use to get buy-in from different departments and stakeholders in the process of launching the program.

3

TOOLS AND APPLICATIONS

TOOLS AND WORKFLOWS FOR MANAGING YOUR TABLETS

Whether they're mounted, used for in-house programs, or loaned out, the tablets in your library are going to see heavy use from staff and patrons. As discussed in the previous chapter, you will need to have policies and workflows in place to manage the information on the tablets, preserve the privacy of user data, and keep tablets running smoothly and securely. Working closely with IT to develop these workflows and conduct any needed staff training will be critical.

One important aspect of managing workflows is having a way to reset your tablets to their default states. This ensures that all users of the tablet have the same access and experience, as well as preserving the privacy of the patron who went before. This is particularly important in the case of circulating tablets that are checked out to individual patrons for extended use.

Setting up a standard user account or profile allows a tablet to return to a predetermined suite of apps and functions that would be common across all tablets, wiping private or accumulated data and allowing for a unified experience across the tablet program. Plan on setting up at least two user profiles for tablets patrons are going to be using: a default Patron profile and a default Staff/Administrator profile. Because apps and settings tailored to children and teens are significantly different from those for adults, plan on creating additional separate accounts and user profiles designated for teen or child tablet users, and keeping those tablets separate. For ease of administering apps and tracking purchases, set up a master library account with the app store you're using, such as the Apple store or Android store, ideally configured as an institutional or educational account. (This makes bulk purchases and updates easier as well.) There are a couple of different options to prevent patrons from making unauthorized purchases on library tablets, including adjusting the control settings in the user profile, or logging out and password-protecting any store accounts. Depending on the level and purpose of your tablets, another option is to reset the tablets completely to factory settings. While this can be a strong safeguard for patron privacy, or a useful fix for a serious technical problem that arises, it will lose any installed apps or other settings you have applied to the tablet and can take a significant amount of time to restore.

In addition to managing the tablet's settings through an account or user profile, there are a number of software applications that allow for the management of multiple devices. While clear communication between IT, access services, and any other department using these tablets is the best strategy when choosing tools and workflows for device management, the following is a brief overview. Both Google Apps for Work and Microsoft 360 are compatible with multiple operating systems. Chromebooks can be configured to link to individual or institutional Google or other e-mail accounts, and can use cloud storage to update and share information across devices. Apple offers Configurator, a program that can manage user profiles, settings, backups, and updates for up to thirty iPads or other iOS devices. The Casper Suite by JAMF software is a paid option for iOS devices. AirWatch can be purchased and used to manage Android devices.

Tablets can be updated by connecting to a main designated computer, updated wirelessly over the network or through the cloud, or in some cases (as in the Google Nexus tablet), updated from a master tablet (by touching the backs of the tablets together). Factors like your library's Internet and wireless bandwidth, the tablet operating systems you choose, and the number and model of your available tablets will determine what method you choose to sync your tablets or restore them to their original settings. Be mindful that updating and resetting virtually can take significantly more time, especially at the library's busiest bandwidth times. If you have a number of tablets that need to update at once, you will want to choose to update them wirelessly or by using a charging cart with sync capability rather than physically connecting each to the designated computer in sequence.

THE APPS

As the saying goes, "there's an app for that." It seems like new apps for tablets and mobile devices are multiplying exponentially every day, ranging in price, quality, purpose, and audience. Keeping track of high-quality apps across the different device platforms your library and patrons are using can feel overwhelming. The organization (or lack thereof) of stores like the iTunes store or the Google Play store for Android, with a difficult search interface that doesn't distinguish between quality apps by established software vendors and homegrown apps created by individuals, only complicates the evaluation and selection process. In addition to selecting apps for library management, programming, and lending, librarians are often cast in the role of "digital media mentors" (Campbell 2014), guiding patrons to select engaging and educational apps for themselves and their children.

Take a deep breath, and let's go back to basics.

App Collection Development

Sourcing apps to outfit your library tablets is, at its heart, collection development. In evaluating and selecting apps for your library and its patrons, you'll be assessing many of the same factors you would in more traditional collection development.

- **Use What You Already Have.** Before moving too far into the array of available app options, plan to outfit your apps with a suite of programs you and your patrons already use on desktop computers, or access through mobile apps. Because they are already familiar to staff and patrons, there is no need for extra research or training. Easy! And possibly cheaper. Check with your existing software licenses and vendors to see how many new tablet devices are covered and what license arrangements might need to be made.

- **Fit with Overall Collection Goals**. Does this app fit with the overall goals of your library and its collections, digital and otherwise? A public library serving predominantly parents and children will want to provide apps that teach and entertain at different educational levels than an academic library serving a population of students and faculty in the sciences.
- **Patron Needs**. What will this app help your patrons do, learn, create, or enjoy? With multimedia and interactive aspects—and functions like being able to create or edit video, set reminders, or track personal progress—apps can help educate, entertain, and motivate patrons in seemingly limitless ways. Be open to app suggestions and learning from your patrons as well.
- **Relationship to Existing Collection**. Apps that emphasize reading and learning can be a good place to start building your collection, but ask yourself: Is this app unique in the needs it fills, the capabilities or information it provides, when compared to the other apps available for download or loaded onto library tablets?
- **Reputation of the Publisher**. Many vendors of content you already know and trust, like Baker & Taylor or OverDrive, have mobile or tablet-friendly app versions of the software you and your patrons have previously used for e-books and audiobooks. Established publishers of educational, creative, and productivity-based software, such as Scholastic or Microsoft, have created tablet versions or additional apps you and your patrons will find useful.
- **Reputation of the Reviewer**. As with other forms of collection development, you can find reviews of new apps in trusted review sources like *Kirkus*, *Library Journal*, *School Library Journal*, and *Publishers Weekly* (good for both adult and children's reviews). To learn about apps for adult patrons and to assist your library's workflow, tech and app reviews from *Business Insider* and *Tech-Crunch* can be good places to start. (See Recommended Reading for a more complete list of resources.)
- **Budget.** Both the Apple store and the Google Play store (for Android apps) offer pricing options for educational institutions, including libraries, to make volume purchases of apps for outfitting multiple devices at once. Another way to structure the funding for purchases of apps is to have individual library branches or

departmental librarians use gift cards for app purchases to outfit individual tablets. In addition to setting aside some funds for app purchases for the library and any tablets that are part of a lending program, you will want to make sure that any tablets set aside for public use, whether onsite in programs or as part of a lending program, have settings controlled so that patrons cannot make app purchases or in-app purchases that could be billed to the library. And remember, even a free app can come with a cost: the time spent with the app will detract from doing some other worthwhile thing.

Collection Development Unique to Apps

Some aspects of app selection differ from traditional collection development in important ways.

- **Relationship to Library Programs.** Because apps provide a hands-on, interactive experience, often with multimedia, using them can be an engaging, even playful, part of library programs and could be built into an event onsite, such as bringing multimedia to a children's storytime, or turning a display in the library into an interactive exploration with augmented reality. A social reading app like Goodreads could become part of forming or running a book group.
- **Recency.** While it's important to select apps that provide updated, relevant information, this can be a case where newer may not always be better. A recently released app runs the risk of not having been debugged yet.
- **Ease of Access and Use.** This consideration differs slightly from traditional selection methods. You want to make sure that the apps you select are easy for their intended audience to use and navigate, with clear instructions and features, and that the technology itself functions smoothly (an interactive storybook doesn't freeze or crash on slow wireless, for example). It's a good idea to take the time to test each app on multiple devices before fully integrating it into the collection or using it as part of a demo.
- **Privacy Management.** While overall guidance about online privacy is part of a librarian's role in teaching digital literacy, issues of

online privacy crop up in relation to tablets that are borrowed from the library or used onsite.

Apps for Specific Patron Populations

While the guidelines above provide a general framework for building and adding to an app collection, there are a few additional guidelines for particular patron populations.

Children and Teens

There are a wealth of educational games, enhanced storybooks, and other apps available that are touted as great apps for children from infancy through their teenage years. The American Academy of Pediatrics advises that children's total entertainment screen time be less than two hours per day (Strasburger et al. 2013). Especially for babies, toddlers, and young children, parents and caregivers need to make sure that any screen time is complementary to the hands-on exploration of the world that enriches children's growth (Lerner and Barr 2013). As media mentors working with parents and teachers, librarians can help ensure that screen time is made of educational and enriching apps that spur active exploration. Demonstrations and guidance in selecting apps gives librarians a chance to expose parents and children to apps that encourage shared learning, social engagement, skill development, and multimedia fun.

While emphasizing apps that offer education, enrichment, and skill development is part of a librarian's role as a curator and mentor, it's also important to remember that games that seem to be just for fun offer learning opportunities as well. Even in a game built for pure entertainment, children are "still learning to use their fingers to direct where they want to go, follow audio and visual cues, and having parallel play, meaning that they are socializing, learning and providing assistance" (S.-A. Taylor 2015).

Curating separate app collections along the lines of age groups, and, if possible, outfitting separate sets of tablets for young children, elementary school, tweens, and teens helps keep the tablet experience age-appropriate as well as enjoyable. Easy-to-navigate apps that emphasize skills like early literacy and reading readiness can be collected on tablets intended for preschool-age children. For school-age children, look for educational apps and games with more complex steps, or subjects and storylines that build on the topics and interests they are learning in school or seeking out for fun. Apps that build games and fun tasks around teaching early coding skills can be good to introduce at the elementary school level, and build on for tweens and teens. For teens and tweens, also consider apps that invite collaboration, media creation, and editing, or integrate with other programs like gaming programs, 3-D printing, graphic design, or makerspace programs that are part of the library's teen programming.

Patrons with Blindness or Low Vision

The audio capacity and adaptive settings of tablets transforms them into a good resource to assist patrons with low vision. Ensure that your app selection includes apps that can have text and images enlarged easily, or configured to provide adaptive audio prompting and guidance for use. Customizations of font size and lighting can make e-reading apps more useful for patrons with low vision. Knowing how to help patrons use voice-activated features on their devices, like Siri for iPhone, can provide valuable assistance as well.

Patrons with Autism

The best strategy for selecting and recommending apps that will be useful and enjoyable for patrons with autism is to work responsively with the individual patrons and caregivers who use your library to recommend apps tailored to meet their specific skill levels, learning goals, and levels of interest. Seek out apps developed and reviewed by educators as fitting specific skill and learning goals, and, if you have any doubts, reach out to ask educators, reviewers, and developers about the app's goals and background research (Mautone 2015). When vetting apps, pay particular attention to the design of the interface; seeking out apps that use cleaner, more streamlined graphics, clearly marked transitions between levels, and apps that have a reliable development history to avoid disruptive crashes, advises Mark Mautone, New Jersey State Teacher of the Year and a lead teacher in the Hoboken Applied Behavior Analysis (ABA) program for educating children with autism. Apps that mimic or use photorealistic depictions of the steps in real-world actions, such as storybooks that use a page-turning motion rather than scrolling, or camera-driven social apps like FaceTime and Skype, can be resources to help you work with patrons with autism and their caregivers because they add specific cues that match real-world experiences. Both scheduling programs that block out chunks of time and programs that offer the ability to sequence or storyboard visuals can help organize and demonstrate steps or sequences of events (Mautone 2015).

Entrepreneurs, Job Seekers, and Small Businesses

Increasingly, libraries of all sizes are becoming centers and resources for business development, whether offering job searching and skills development, support and education for business growth, financial planning resources, collaborative meeting spaces, or tools like 3-D printers, graphics programs, or media centers to help solopreneurs and small businesses learn and innovate. Curating selections of apps for budgeting, financial planning, productivity, and document sharing will enhance programming offerings to help small, mobile businesses and entrepreneurs of all interests. Library programming and app selection focused on graphic design, photo editing, web development, or even strategies for blogging and social media management could draw budding creative entrepreneurs. If the library is part of a school with a strong art and design or computer programming course program, work with subject specialist librarians, and even in partnership with the departments themselves, to build app selections and library programming of interest.

Presentations about crafting a resume that displays well on mobile devices, as well as using smart, targeted keywords to improve search visibility, could be shared using tablets plugged into projection screens for group displays. Apps that teach skills from coding to app development to language could also help candidates strengthen their search.

Publicizing Your App Collection

As patrons explore your tablets, whether in-house or borrowed, they will encounter and ask questions about the app collections you've curated. Showcase new apps on your mounted tablets and build them into storytimes or other nontablet programs. Make an Appy Hour presentation of eight to ten apps on a theme, using a projection screen to present a five- to ten-minute walkthrough of each app's key features, followed by time for patrons to try the app loaded onto library tablets.

Share the lists of apps as handouts and post on your library's website and social media afterward.

Teaching and advising patrons about the tablet apps that will serve their needs is, at its heart, advisory service. By selecting and presenting apps, librarians are fulfilling a role as media mentors and providing "appvisory" services using the same principles.

See? Not *that* overwhelming after all.

4

LIBRARY EXAMPLES AND CASE STUDIES

From large public library systems to subject-specific elementary school projects, libraries are already beginning to put the potential of tablets into practice. Some libraries are using tablets to streamline and enhance library operations and staff workflows. Others are using multimedia tools to offer enhanced versions of traditional library programming or new learning experiences to build digital literacy. Lending tablets and devices gives patrons an enhanced experience of digital media and productivity tools. Tablets on display in the library space invite hands-on exploration and curiosity about library resources and programs, guided by patrons' own pace and interests.

Public and academic libraries use tablets to offer ready access to e-resources, offer opportunities to experiment with new digital possibilities, and enhance traditional library programs. Academic libraries at all levels and subject specialties use digital reference resources and subject-specific apps to extend learning and harness the tools of the flipped classroom. While emerging technologies librarians working closely with IT departments often take the lead in developing and implementing tablet programs, librarians of all specialties can take the lead on a tablet project; and coordinating across departments is key, as well as finding ways to foster larger partnerships.

No matter whether your library matches the shape, size, and audience of the libraries in the following examples, they can provide insights into devising and managing tablet programs for a variety of audiences.

TABLETS FOR STAFF TRAINING

Choosing the Right Device: The Nielsen Library at Adams University

Whether choosing a device and platform for staff use or patron-facing programs, many of the considerations are the same. Choose a device that will integrate into any existing system architecture and allow you to meet patron needs and carry out the tasks of library operations as efficiently as possible. These are some of the factors that led Stacy Taylor, emerging technologies librarian of the Nielsen Library at Adams State University in Alamosa, Colorado, to advocate Chromebooks for staff use. The process she used to persuade library administration to adopt Chromebooks, and to train staff to integrate them into practice, is informative to any librarian seeking staff and administrative buy-in for device and platform adoption, no matter what the specific device and platform.

The Chromebooks used by the Nielsen Library staff support a robust technology lending program. Students, faculty, and staff are able to

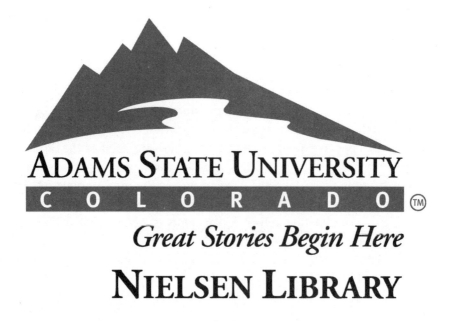

Figure 4.1.   Nielsen Library at Adams State University Logo

borrow laptops, Nooks, Kindle Fire and Kindles, Nexus 7 tablets, Microsoft Surface RT tablets, and Chromebooks, as well as cameras and equipment, GPS devices, and Raspberry Pi and Arduino programmable devices.

While the initial plan had been to acquire iPads for staff use, Stacy Taylor suggested Chromebooks as an alternative. To allow the staff the experience of comparing the two devices, Taylor provided basic training in operating the Chromebooks, then sent each staffer a list of tasks to complete with each device—basic things that were part of a normal workflow: checking e-mail and calendars, creating and sharing a Google Doc, taking notes in meetings. After spending a week with each device, each staffer took a short survey Taylor designed. "We determined that the Chromebooks were better for work-related purposes, whereas the iPad was a fun device better for consumption of media. (S. Taylor 2015). The other factors Taylor felt made a case for the Chromebooks were its keyboard, integration with the Google apps already heavily used in the library's system, compatibility with the Chromeboxes running the library's OPACs, ease of updating, the ability to use the cloud to make information accessible between tablet devices (especially useful for multiple users on the same tablet), and the existing support from the IT department.

The library purchased Chromebooks in February of 2014. The library has eight Chromebooks, one for each staffer, to be used for managing daily tasks, conducting roving reference, sharing information at conferences, and staying in touch when out of the office. The Computing Services department required the purchase of a management license for the Chromebooks, which allows administration to manage setup tasks such as configuring e-mail access, session limits, media preferences, data storage, and being able to track missing devices.

The Takeaway: Encouraging staff to compare devices in hands-on testing that mirrors their regular tasks can be an effective way to elicit buy-in to a proposed program. (And could be adapted to launching a patron program, too!)

Building and Evaluating Your Program: The Cedar Rapids Public Library

The Cedar Rapids Public Library has two branches serving the town of Cedar Rapids, Indiana. The library began a lending program circulating Google Nexus tablets and LeapPad tablets for children in February 2014. The program, to buy two sets of tablets, one for children and one for adults, was spearheaded by the library director and funded through a combination of the library budget and donations from the local Kiwanis Club and ITC Midwest (Hanel 2015).

To plan the program, the Cedar Rapids Public Library researched and contacted other libraries with tablet programs, finding that the majority of libraries they contacted made tablets available for in-house use rather than lending (Hanel 2015). Library staff conducted hands-on testing and discussion of different tablet models and types to reach the decision to purchase Google Nexus tablets for the adult programs and LeapPad devices for children. Staff also designated a cabinet where tablets could be displayed and secured under lock and key, and purchased cases that were custom-printed with the library logo for circulating tablets.

Cedar Rapids chose the Google Nexus tablet because of its screen size, customizability, and the price point for its features. LeapPad

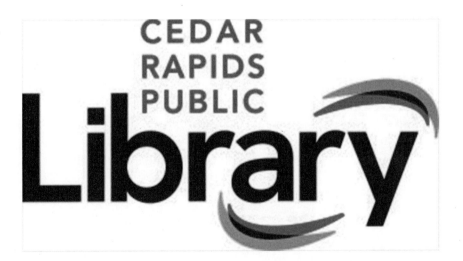

Figure 4.2.   Cedar Rapids Library Logo

Ultras were chosen, out of a sparser selection of children's tablet options, because they seemed durable and offered a reasonable variety of educational content (Hanel 2015).

Nexus tablets circulate with mobile app versions of the services to which the library already subscribes, including Zinio, OverDrive, Freegal, and 3M. Demand for the circulating tablets was so high from the moment the program launched with fifty Nexus tablets that the library decided to purchase fifty more to satisfy patron demand (Hanel 2015). Reference librarian Trevor Hanel praises the ease of wiping the Nexus device between patrons, a five-minute process using a flash drive configured by the library's IT department, and adds that the process of charging the devices is much more time-consuming.

Since the program began, Hanel notes that wear and tear and theft of the devices have been the main areas of concern. Within the first ten months of the program, over a quarter of the LeapPad Ultra devices had sustained damage that couldn't be attributed to any one patron; and that several of them were stolen before the procedure of keeping the tablets in a locked display cabinet was instituted. To remedy issues of theft and damage of Nexus devices, the library used circulation data to determine how to strengthen use restrictions. By restricting Nexus borrowing privileges to library card holders who were permanent town residents with no outstanding fines, damage to the devices was decreased dramatically.

The Takeaway: Reach out and learn from other libraries' programs. Use partnerships to secure funding. Build consensus with staff. Assess borrowing patterns to confront and remedy obstacles through changes to security policies and operations.

Traditional and Digital Literacy with the iPad: L.E. Phillips Memorial Library

The L.E. Phillips Memorial Public Library in Eau Claire, Wisconsin, launched its iPad program in 2011, in partnership with the Presto Foundation. The Presto Foundation wanted to fund iPads and develop a lending program as assistive technology to allow patrons with low vision to continue reading (Small 2015) and to build digital literacy and device experience for the larger community. The library director and staffers worked with the Presto Foundation to establish a plan for the

Figure 4.3.   L.E. Phillips Memorial Library Logo

project, and also consulted with the city attorney to determine the legality of the project and procedures. The goal for implementation was to make iPads available with preloaded content but also allow patrons to use their own iTunes accounts to download apps and content as needed.

The first step was to have a thorough understanding of the kinds of decisions that would need to be made, and by whom, and how the steps and issues should be addressed. The library established subcommittees devoted to policy, technology, packaging, cataloging, and PR concurrently, under the umbrella of the Presto iPad Endeavor (PIE) committee (Small 2015). The PIE committee planned the policies and procedures for all aspects of the proposed tablet program, including borrower eligibility, how content would be selected and added to the devices, and how patron privacy would be preserved between borrowers.

At the time the program launched, there were few options for storage carts for multiple devices, which made the selection of the Bretford charging cart they still use today straightforward. Experimentation with different procedures and approaches on her own time played a key role for Isa Small, programming and communications service manager, in establishing a workflow for updating and maintaining devices between patron uses. Because the program was launched prior to the advent of the iCloud, all of the devices needed to be managed from one central computer and iTunes account. Using iTunes, the library set up a Master Backup for all the iPads. When borrowed iPads are returned, they are reset completely to factory settings before having e-books and apps reloaded from the institutional Master Backup. However, as Small observed, relying on the iCloud to restore takes significantly longer than connecting them to a computer.

When the program began, the library anticipated a higher demand for in-house iPad use, but found that the majority of patrons wanted to take the device home (Miller 2015), so they reduced the number of in-house iPads to two. Increasing the lending period from seven to fourteen days and integrating the devices into the library's existing home delivery lending also helped meet patron needs. Contrary to the conventional wisdom of many libraries that increases the deployment of devices after a small pilot program, the L.E. Phillips Library found it easier to manage the device program with a smaller number of iPads than originally planned. After launching with twenty-eight iPads available on a seven-day loan, with a holds queue that topped out at 450, Circulation Manager Laura Miller decided that there were far too many devices to manage sensibly and shifted to circulating only ten iPad Air devices (Miller 2015). Miller manages the holds queue list to assure that demand and lending criteria are met. Managing the program over several years, Miller has noted that the same handful of patrons appear on the holds list as repeat borrowers.

The Takeaway: It bears repeating: planning and partnerships are key. Make sure to assess the staff workload in tandem with hold and circulation data in evaluating how to improve the lending program.

Circulating and Managing a Wide Range of Devices: The Dover Town Library

The Dover Town Library, serving a community of six thousand in the town of Dover, Massachusetts, loans a number of different types of tablets, as part of a robust and unique lending program that includes, says Library Director Cheryl Abdullah-Abouelaziz, "everything from tablets to e-readers to gaming consoles to carpet steamers. I had someone call us to ask for a concrete driller once. We didn't have one, but it made me happy to know that the library was the place they thought to ask" (Abdullah-Abouelaziz 2015). The tablet lending program launched in 2010, beginning when Abdullah-Abouelaziz watched the World Cup and realized the ubiquity of digital and mobile technology helping people in rural villages access information and stay connected.

Because the library is small, with a staff of ten, most of the decisions about creating and launching the program were made collaboratively. To provide the widest range of access and learning opportunities, the library determined to purchase multiple devices and operating systems, selecting devices at the 32 GB storage range, with enough processing power to support media streaming and support the average patron's needs, rather than the processing power needed for business endeavor (Abdullah-Abouelaziz 2015). After researching the available devices, comparing prices and features, seeking the highest processing power and stability for the investment, and knowing they would be downloading e-books, the program began with Kindle because Amazon was easy to work with. Because the Kindle program was an immediate success, the library decided to add six iPads. The iPads were so immediately popular that the library doubled the number in a matter of weeks and went up to 110 iPads just three months later (Abdullah-Abouelaziz 2015). They continue to add devices as new ones hit the stores, buying at least six, and then adding more in response to user interest. The one exception so far has been the Nook, which was not in as high demand and so topped out at twelve. Keeping the device program varied and responsive to patron requests "provides the community with an opportunity to have a leveled playing field through digital access to build digital literacy. It was changing so rapidly at first that individuals couldn't keep up," Abdullah-Abouelaziz said. In recognition of the library's commitment to digital literacy and access, the library won a $10,000 grant from the Bill and Melinda Gates Foundation in 2012.

The small size of the staff means that everyone is cross-trained to update and manage the multiple devices; they also have a stake in decision-making about new purchases and programs. To make sure that the entire staff had the same level of experience working closely with devices in library operations and everyday life, Abdullah-Abouelaziz used a portion of the grant money to purchase iPod Touch devices for the entire staff. One-on-one or in small groups, the staff were trained to use the devices for QR code scanning, app recommendations, patron training, searching catalogs and the stacks, taking pictures and uploading to the library's social media, and learning to stream video (Abdullah-Abouelaziz 2015). Personalized training with the devices, Abdullah-Abouelaziz observed, "really made a difference for staff confidence using technology and helping patrons."

Tablets are available for patron use on stands in the main library and the children's library. Tablets showcasing topical content like e-books or magazines to browse are on stands near the relevant shelves of books in the library, to draw interest and invite browsing of both physical and electronic resources. Tablets for checkout are located behind the circulation desk. According to library policy, none of the technology or the library's other unique lending items can be placed on hold. Patrons can come into the library to borrow devices for a period of three weeks, not eligible for renewals. Some of the iPads are preloaded with a selection of e-books and some are loaded with a selection of magazines (Abdullah-Abouelaziz 2015).

Some of the loaner iPads are configured as early literacy iPads with kid-friendly apps. Children gravitate toward the wall-mounted iPads loaded with apps for demonstrations all over the library. Librarians also use tablets for e-book storytimes. The library logs out of the institutional ID before lending devices and wipes patron data upon return to ensure privacy, using an Apple Air as the central computer to maintain and update the default patron profile (Abdullah-Abouelaziz 2015).

Word of mouth has consistently spread news of the device program and new additions. "The exceptional stuff promotes itself. We still work to promote traditional library services and programs," Abdullah-Abouelaziz notes.

One issue Abdullah-Abouelaziz and her fellow librarians have noted in managing the lending program for devices and other unique objects is in cataloging and managing circulation data. The Dover Town Library is part of a consortium that uses a library management system that simply does not have wide enough categories to catalog and track data for the range of items in Dover's collection. To resolve this issue, the library began using BiblioBoard to catalog and process circulation for its unique items. Library patrons can log into BiblioBoard using their library accounts to explore the collection of technology and other unique devices on offer. But, in a small and friendly town library, they are more likely to just come in and ask, says Abdullah-Abouelaziz.

The Takeaway: Build staff training that incorporates daily device use rather than a few demonstrations. When you're getting ready to implement a device program, be aware that cataloging diverse or unique items can pose a challenge. Work closely with your catalogers and have a good understanding of the options and procedures of your integrated library management system (ILMS), or that of any consortium your library belongs to.

Serving a Diverse Patron Population with a Unified User Experience: The Queens Public Library

The borough of Queens in New York City is home to one of the most culturally and linguistically diverse patron populations of any library system in the United States. To support the immigrant communities thriving around each of its branches, the library collects materials in a variety of languages (Berger 2012). In October of 2012, several Queens neighborhoods, most notably the Rockaways, were devastated by storm damage from Hurricane Sandy. Many homes and businesses were destroyed and entire neighborhoods were left without power (Epps and Watson 2014). During the emergency, several libraries in the system were forced to close to repair damage, while those that were able to do so remained open to assist the community.

In 2013, Google partnered with New York State to make a donation of five thousand Google Nexus tablets to the Queens Library system, to be rolled out first in the seven branches most affected by Hurricane Sandy, before being rolled out system-wide in the summer of 2015 (Watson 2015). The donation from Google determined the number and type of the tablets, while decisions about administration, content, and distribution of the tablets was a collaboration across multiple departments in the library, particularly IT, Technical Services, Collection Development, and Public Services.

From the start, the central philosophy of the Queens Library tablet program was to make the tablets be a virtual library resource and extension of the library rather than a separate device, and to use existing processes and content wherever possible to manage the tablet program.

Figure 4.4.   Queens Library Logo

"We make it part of other programs. We try not to treat it like a separate program," said Kelvin Watson, director of E-Content and Strategy (Watson 2015). From an operations standpoint, this meant building the distribution of tablets into the existing system using the same trucks and delivery procedures in place for interlibrary loan. The policies for the program carried over from those already established for lending digital content and devices, such as the wireless hotspots the library lends, sometimes in tandem with tablets. Patrons can borrow a device for one month, and can renew to a period of four total months. The Queens Library added the new tablets to the existing customer service workflows and programs already in place to train branch personnel in new procedures and new technology, combining onsite staff training and demonstrations with manuals and IT support as they had with past device innovations (Watson 2015).

For the tablets themselves, this meant focusing on creating a tablet experience that would work for the entire patron base, young and old, tech-savvy and tech novice, and leveraging already licensed content, using existing vendor partnerships and licenses to populate the tablets with access to e-books using existing Axis 360 and OverDrive licenses, magazines from Zinio, and free music downloads from Freegal. Managing preloaded content so closely tied to the mission of the library focuses on the tablet as a content resource rather than a tool (Watson 2015). The tablets provide educational resources such as database access to assist learners at all levels. The tablet has been integrated into GED programs, adult literacy programs, and used by patrons completing college degrees. The library uses the AirWatch mobile device management system to lock down the tablets and limit patron access to games. However, Watson observes, "people are borrowing it for specific resources, not for the playing of games. Tech-savvy patrons could, potentially, circumvent that, but the majority of the people borrowing the device aren't interested in hacking the devices."

An important part of making the tablets a seamless extension of the library's content and programming has been to go beyond getting the licenses and lending tablets to focusing on creating a better and more accessible library experience (Watson 2015). The core of the Queens Library tablet experience is the API (Application Programming Interface), designed by the library's team of in-house developers and programmers. Integrating vendor content into their own custom-designed

Figure 4.5.   Circulating tablets at the Queens Library (Image courtesy of Queens Library)

in-house API means showcasing and curating content with an understanding of what libraries and patrons want, rather than prioritizing the vendors. Rather than introducing a new e-book reading platform, working with existing vendor partnerships represents a more practical approach. The library is designing ways to make the customer experience of vendor content better with techniques such as presenting a visually coherent design across the different capabilities of the tablet and streamlining the steps involved in discovery and download of media. Looking toward the future, Watson observes that he would like to see an even more consolidated virtual library experience, with even more unified search and discovery, better indexing and better ways of facilitating exploring, generating results across both physical and virtual resources (Watson 2015).

The Queens Library tablet program has been publicized in-house through signage and displays and through integration into live library programming, such as computer and literacy classes and other educational programs. Because of its innovative API, numerous libraries and library organizations have recognized the ways the Queens Library has capitalized on digital technology for its tablet program and for its mobile app, which is compatible across Apple and Android platforms. Queens librarians have given presentations at ALA and state conferences and have been invited to speak at library consortia groups and the Innovative Interfaces Directors Meeting.

The Takeaway: While access to a large in-house team of developers to create a custom API gives the Queens Library an advantage not every library has, libraries of any size using tablets can draw a few important lessons: Add tablets into existing programs and workflows rather than starting from scratch. Populate devices with apps that draw on the library's existing vendor partnerships. Offer apps in a user interface that looks and feels as coherent as possible to navigate. Test individual tablet operations and apps to make sure that the user interface is as streamlined and easy to use as possible.

TABLET PROGRAMS FOR CHILDREN

Tailoring a tablet program to children and teens, whether through a public library's children's department or through a school, capitalizes on both the richness of existing traditional models for children's programming and the enhancements of drawing on multimedia and apps by using tablets.

Choosing the Right Tablet for Student Patrons: The Ferguson Municipal Public Library

When planning a tablet program, partnerships with stakeholders can offer guidance to shape the purpose and audience of the program as well as a welcome source of funding. However, it's important to do your own research to compare device and hardware functionalities and, especially, prices, to make sure to select the right tech and hardware for your specific use case.

The Ferguson Library, funded in part by The Missouri Chapter of Links Incorporated, acquired ten tablets and associated hardware as part of a program to provide after school instruction and mentorship resources available to to students from Cool Valley Elementary School. The program, launched in October of 2014, developed as a part-

Figure 4.6.   Ferguson Library Logo

nership between the school, Links Inc. and the Ferguson Municipal Library, aims to help students to learn and develop skills using resources available through Khan Academy, a nonprofit that offers online multimedia educational resources at no cost.

While the initial plan budgeted for the purchase of ten Chromebooks for the program, Scott Bonner, director of the Ferguson Municipal Library District, advocated Google Nexus 7 tablets as a better alternative. He championed Google Nexus tablets for the program for a number of reasons. He advocated for the tablets over laptops because providing an opportunity for students to become more familiar with working with tablets and their touch screens would "help bridge the digital divide in a more forward-thinking way" (Bonner 2015). The functionality and flexibility of tablets make them the hallmark of future tech trends, Bonner said. He praised the features and capabilities of the Nexus tablets as well. Administration through Google Apps for Education is straightforward (Bonner 2015). Google for Education and the Nexus system offer embedded security settings and features that can be locked down securely to place limits on how users can access and change the system. Restoring the settings of a Nexus tablet is a simple process that takes a matter of minutes. One tablet is set up as a master tablet with the default features and apps. Tablets can be restored to the master settings simply by touching their backs together, after which tablets will be restored in a matter of minutes. Also, the Nexus tablets and their hardware were determined to be more affordable. Using the same amount of money that the Links organization had initially earmarked for the program, Bonner was able to purchase ten Google Nexus 7 tablets, a Belkin cart to store and charge them, and tethering and locks to secure tablets when they were checked out for use. After the tablets were purchased and outfitted with peripheral resources, Bonner had money left in reserve. The initial plan from Links envisioned the tablets as being secured by being docked securely on tabletop stands with hardware. Bonner expressed concern that fixing the tablets to the tables would take up valuable table space and reduce the functionality of the tablets (Bonner 2015). Instead, he proposed an alternate security mechanism of tethering cords. Using Kensington Desktop Locking Kit and Desktop Mini-Plate anchor, the tablet being used could be both mobile and secure. The cords have about four feet of range, Bonner noted, allowing patrons to use the tablet more naturally, by holding it in their laps, or being able to sprawl in the comfy chairs in the library (Bonner 2015).

Once launched, the program was publicized by Links organization members conducting classroom presentations at Cool Valley. As of this writing, Cool Valley students and their mentors, the program's intended audience, have not used the library as a meeting spot, or checked out the tablets in the library. Future plans for the tablet program, Bonner surmised, could include expanding a wider tablet lending program (Bonner 2015). If made available to the wider Ferguson Library community, priority would still be given to its original intended audience, the Cool Valley Elementary School students and their mentors using Khan Academy software during after school hours. Repurposed for more widespread availability, Bonner is confident that publicizing it with signage in the library, mentions across library social media, and word of mouth in the community would lead to high demand for the tablets, and that the tablet lending program will publicize itself (Bonner 2015).

The Takeaway: Choose your operating system based on the cost, relative to the functions and ways your target population will use it.

Tablets Tailored for Ages and Stages: The Children's Library at Darien Library

As part of a device lending program that includes 21-day loans of Nook and Sony e-Readers loaded with a selection of books, and iPads for the use of patrons of all ages, the Darien Library in Darien, Connecticut, uses loaner tablets and in-house technology in support of two programs of particular interest for children's librarians and school librarians: Early Literacy and Tween Tablets. Six iPads are set up with apps to promote Early Literacy for young children and parents. There are four Tween Tablets available as part of the Darien Library TEA Room, a mini-makerspace program offering children in grades 3 through 6 opportunities to explore traditional arts and crafts classes and projects like printmaking, as well as circuitry and programming with Raspberry Pi, for example. Early Literacy iPad kits blend technology together with best practices in Early Literacy to promote literacy and prereading skills (Moore 2015). Three tablets are available for in-library use, mounted on tables with hardware from MacLocks. The in-house tablets help

Figure 4.7.   Darien Library Logo

build interest in circulating tablets and provide a place to test well-reviewed new apps the library is considering adding to the suite available on loaner iPads.

The Takeaway: Use the tablets to enhance exploration and experimentation in your library and to enhance library programs. Setting up tablets for different ages and stages is also a good plan.

Tablets, "Appvisory," and Outreach: The Pasadena Public Library

Youth services librarians at the Pasadena Public Library in Pasadena, California, are noteworthy for savvy in-library programming to help parents and children learn about age-appropriate, quality apps, as well as for the outreach they do to promote the apps as part of their educational programming. Using tablets linked to projection screens, they present apps as part of programs and conclude each program with a handout for families to take with them for reference (Driscoll, Hurtado, and Rojo 2014).

For children aged three to five and their caregivers, Pasadena librarians present eStorytime. eStorytime combines traditional storytime activities like sing-alongs and movement with quality children's books enhanced for iPad (Sun 2014).

Appy Hour presentations for school-age children and caregivers use ten iPads (one linked to a projector for staff demonstrations, and nine available for children and caregivers to use in turn) for demonstrations and descriptions of eight to ten apps organized around a central theme, like STEM (science, technology, engineering, and math) apps for elementary schoolers. Librarians use a projector to demonstrate a walk-through of the selection of apps, and then provide hands-on demonstration time for children and caregivers to explore each one.

In addition to building live in-library programs around apps, the library has developed Pinterest boards archiving past app recommendations, grouped along the same age categories. Other Pinterest boards offer educational resources about children's digital literacy and media consumption to aid parents. Pasadena has done a terrific job of adapting existing social media resources to provide rich, ready reference in a shareable and appealing format.

The Takeaway: Practice with the apps yourself before using them to enhance live programs. Use a combination of hands-on experience, paper handouts, and social media to provide resources and publicize the program. When presenting programs for children, capitalize on the ways multimedia can enhance education, play, and exploration.

While each of these programs is tailored to the educational and entertainment needs of school-age children, the process behind programming and app selection can provide insights for libraries of any size or potential audience. Build tablets and apps into existing programs by finding quality topical apps that invite further exploration while building digital literacy skills. Extend your role as a librarian to be a media mentor, providing targeted appvisory services. Use the free tools of social media as an easy way to promote your services and extend the availability of your app recommendations.

TABLETS IN ACADEMIC LIBRARIES

Early Adoption of Tablets at an Engineering School: The NCSU Library

"What a library does well is provide access to resources that no one person can purchase on their own, but can use and enjoy through collective access to shared resources," says David Woodbury, the associate head of user experience for North Carolina State University at Raleigh (Woodbury 2015). The NCSU Library, Woodbury says, embraced early adoption of tablet technology as central to the library's overall goals. The program was developed and launched quickly, by purchasing iPads at a store to give to student bloggers to test and getting ready to implement them in the program. The early launch of the program with student bloggers generated a lot of publicity, both on campus and in the media, for the device program as a whole, even while it was developing. "We're all about providing the tools people want to use," Woodbury says, adding that the library planned to let their understanding of the iPad's potential as an academic tool evolve as the program developed.

Early adoption of a device program makes sense for the NCSU Library system because it's a central part of the university's overall mission. Like the makerspace program running out of the Hunt Library

Figure 4.8.   NCSU Library Logo

on the NCSU campus, providing access to devices relates back to the central goals of the NCSU academic program. "Because we're an engineering school, we can train the engineers, innovators, entrepreneurs of tomorrow," says Woodbury. "And they need access to the latest technology. That means they can do cool things, learn and build cool apps, and that's part of NCSU's overall competitive advantage" (Woodbury 2015).

The library's iPad program is run primarily out of the Access and Delivery Services Department. Librarians in User Experience select the technology and work on the web representation to improve outreach by promoting the devices on the library's web and social media presence. User Experience and IT collaborated to figure out how to deal with security aspects with regard to patron data, says Woodbury, noting that there aren't really any satisfactory enterprise tools to wipe patron data, and that Erase All Content works, decently, to reset iPads between patrons. Cataloging and Access and Delivery Services set up the cataloging and discovery for the iPads, creating a separate category for iPads in their system. Funding for the upkeep of the program comes through an ongoing technology fund (Woodbury 2015).

The NCSU program currently circulates fifty iPad devices of various generations, replacing them each year as devices break or wear out. Older devices are circulated for seven days, while newer devices circulate for a period of four hours. The library recently launched a program to lend out four Specialty iPads along with an iPad-compatible Structural Scanner that can be used to scan rooms and make architectural models (Woodbury 2015). The Specialty iPads are extremely popular with the library's makerspace program. The library also circulates six Microsoft Surface tablets and twelve Google Nexus tablets, to support a growing interest in developing Android apps. To keep interest in the device program high, device show-and-tell is woven into library instruction. Devices are on display in cabinets and some are mounted on display tables available for free demonstration (Woodbury 2015).

NCSU staff use tablets to complete library tasks, including roving reference and data collection with regard to library resources and space use. They have created their own open-source mobile app, called Suma, which is a great tool for tracking data like reference interactions and headcounts in library spaces (NCSU Libraries 2014).

With the exception of the Specialty iPads, the loaner tablets are outfitted only with the default applications, and users are able to customize whatever apps they need during the loan period, which is important to support a program that all students and staff are eligible to use across the campus, regardless of school or department or disciplinary affiliation. While the library initially used Configurator for maintenance of some of its iPad devices, they now use Casper as their device management system (Woodbury 2015). One snag that NCSU has noted in the lending process is one that other libraries profiled here have reported: passcodes and passwords. Sometimes, when a user sets an activation lock or password, the library has to contact the last user to undo it.

While other libraries (and indeed, some of the guidance in the Getting Started chapter of this very book) might stress the importance of meticulous planning prior to a slowly measured launch for a device lending program, Woodbury and the NCSU library offer a successful example of embracing the opposite approach, moving swiftly to create access and building the program as they went. The fact that they had the support network of a large university infrastructure contributed to their success. But a library doesn't need to be part of a large university, or even cater to a thriving population of engineers, entrepreneurs, and innovators, to succeed with a relatively quick progression into a lending program. Being able to justify the program as deeply ingrained in the library's goals of patron service, in an essential way, is the key. It also helps to have solid financial resources, a willingness to work across departments, and a willingness to experiment.

Stay Responsive to Patron Needs: The Martin Luther King Jr. Library at SJSU

The story of the tablet lending program at the Martin Luther King, Jr. Library at San Jose State University in California is one of smart planning and implementation, as well as the evolution of patron needs. Before starting the program, says Farrukh Farid, IT manager at the library, library faculty and staff looked to other libraries' programs for inspiration and guidance, visiting libraries in the California State University (CSU) and University of California (UC) systems to see how they were handling their device lending programs (Farid 2015). When they saw that other libraries in the system were loaning iPads as well as laptops, they decided to do the same. University Purchasing had the library purchase the devices through the campus bookstore, along with screen protectors and smart covers and an iMac, the designated imaging server, using iTunes to restore the tablets to the default library settings (Farid 2015). Looking back on the purchases, Farid observed that the smart covers were a valuable purchase, while the screen protectors were less so, because students tended to remove them entirely or replace them improperly, trapping bubbles underneath. While Farid praises the cart they purchased from Anthro as "the perfect cart for iPads," he notes that they needed to purchase an extra set of power adapters because the ones in the cart were permanently attached.

At the launch of the program, with the purchase of twenty-six iPads, Farid led a presentation to familiarize staff and faculty with the devices. Enthusiasm was fueled, he said, by the devices being the latest rage. Since then, updating staff knowledge has been a matter of learning from one another, whether through informal questions or more structured lunch-and-learn training session presentations demonstrating the tools of the iPad or using it as part of a more topical presentation (Farid 2015). Farid attributes the relatively slow uptake of the iPad technology among staff to "technology shyness that slowly evolved into curiosity and experimentation." As the program has gone on, however, Farid noted that staff interest in the iPads has begun to wane, and that the five iPads designated for staff are not used as often. Student Computing Services, a subdivision of Access Services, is in charge of the device lending program that includes iPads and a selection of laptops. The initial iPad lending period of four hours proved to be unpopular with students, so the library added a seven-day lending option, which was very well received. The library's IT division handles any technical issues that arise (Farid 2015).

To determine what apps to load onto the iPads, Farid researched what other universities were offering and decided not to emulate the universities that offered hundreds of apps on loaner devices. Instead, he used his judgment to create a selection including Dropbox, Google apps, Prezi, social media applications like Twitter, a few different e-reading apps, Dictionary, Red Laser (a barcode and QR reader), Hoku-sai (an audio editor), a graphing calculator, WebEx, iTunesU, Skitch, and MindMeister among others (Farid 2015).

When borrowed iPads are returned, they are checked for physical damage, then wiped and erased completely, before being reimaged using iTunes and restored to the library's default settings and apps. If necessary, the borrower is held accountable for significant damage, such as a bent or broken frame, a broken screen, foreign objects broken off in the headphone jack, or damage to the power cables (Farid 2015). Although damage to newer devices is covered by AppleShare, expensive repairs to older damaged devices are not covered, leading to some uncertainty about the fate of the devices.

As other libraries profiled in these pages have described, the SJSU library has had some issues with users adding passcodes, or locking the iPads. Farid acknowledges the dilemma between offering the least re-strictive access possible (both to provide a seamless user experience and to remove the enticement of working around the challenge of restric-tions) and incorporating a level of management that would reduce the instance of devices being locked this way. This limitation in Apple's management tools, Farid says, means that the only option is to contact the last borrower to unlock the system with their user credentials.

While it is an inconvenience, it's a rare enough problem that Farid doesn't describe it as a deal breaker; he is optimistic that moving to Configurator for overall device management will help resolve the problem.

The device lending program has always been self-promoting, Farid says, and the newest devices, the latest Mac laptops, are so highly coveted that they disappear almost as soon as they are returned (Farid 2015). There has been less interest in borrowing iPads than in other devices, especially recently. Once the novelty wore off, iPads were not nearly as sought after as other devices in the library. "Borrowers do not see the iPad as a serious computing device" to support their academic work, Farid says, noting that students will choose to check out a Mac-Book Pro or Windows laptop, and even an older, battered Windows laptop over an iPad for serious study or work in the library. As damaged iPads come out of warranty, Farid and the library have been faced with a decision: whether to repair or replace the iPads, or begin incorporating different devices, such as Android tablets or Chromebooks.

The Takeaway: The SJSU lending program illustrates a principle that is central to any device lending program: both technology and user needs are going to evolve over time. The inevitable need to replace devices offers an opportunity to reevaluate how your library's selection of devices is meeting patron needs.

Tablets in a Medical Library: The Arizona Health Sciences Library

As more aspects of medical practice and health record-keeping become electronic, medical schools and hospitals are launching programs using tablets as part of education and training. To help support digital information-seeking behavior and training, medical libraries are beginning to incorporate more tablet use into their programming and circulation offerings. As the case of the Arizona Health Sciences Library illustrates,

Figure 4.9. Arizona Health Sciences Library Logo

some of the planning considerations and workflows involved in launching a tablet program in a medical library parallel those faced by any library: choosing devices and planning a workflow that will allow for staff training and the support of patron goals and needs. Because of the implementation of an iPad program for incoming medical students at the University of Arizona College of Medicine's Tucson campus in 2011 and the already widespread use of iPads among existing medical students, the library decided to launch an iPad circulation program of its own. Emerging technologies librarian Nicole Capdarest-Arest led the program through strategizing, program development, training, and policy writing to support it, with some input from the library director. Having tablets available allowed for exploration and experimentation to familiarize students and faculty with the technology. It also provided support and backup for students who had questions about accessing resources or even needed something as simple as borrowing a device on the way to class (Capdarest-Arest 2013). In addition to the default suite of apps, the loaner tablets included productivity apps such as Dropbox and Evernote, social media apps, numerous reading apps such as Kindle, Adobe, and CourseSmart (a textbook-reader app), tools for managing reference and citations, and a complement of medical reference apps, some of which were already part of the library's existing subscriptions. The medical apps included 3D Brain, DynaMed, Agency for Healthcare Research and Quality, PloS Reader, and numerous others (Capdarest-Arest 2013).

A key factor in ensuring the program's success was to purchase iPads for staff use. All of the liaison librarians were provided with tablets, as well as information desk librarians and staff, and key personnel in collection services and access services (Capdarest-Arest 2015). Having their own work experience with iPads helped staff prepare to answer student questions. Although the program was always small in size, with up to five circulating iPads at one campus library, Capdarest-Arest notes that the training in procedures of wiping and resetting loaned devices between patrons was the most labor-intensive part of launching the program (2015). It required significant investment of training time at the outset, as well as continued monitoring to ensure that staff conducted all the steps of wiping and resetting the devices between patrons.

The Cleveland Clinic Alumni Library: Secure Tablets for Hospital Workers

The Cleveland Clinic Alumni Library is a medical library primarily serving the information needs of hospital employees at the Cleveland Clinic and has a small device lending program of five iPads, primarily loaned to doctors (fellows and residents), research assistants, and some nurses (Kraft 2015). The circulating iPads are especially useful in the hospital environment because they are configured to access the hospital's secure network, unlike any staff member's personal devices. Doctors and other medical personnel use iPads heavily for work tasks and research, but due to patient privacy regulations (HIPAA), personal devices cannot access the hospital network, so a personal device on the hospital premises would be no different than a doctor using an iPad to treat patients from home (Kraft 2015).

Planning to launch her library's iPad lending program, Michelle Kraft, senior medical librarian, turned to other medical and academic libraries for advice and examples to use as guides. In developing the program, she worked closely with both hospital administration and IT to find a way to make the program meet both the functionality and privacy requirements of the hospital system. Purchasing iPads and licenses for them through the library and the hospital allowed the devices to connect securely to the hospital network and allowed doctors, nurses, and other caregivers to access patient medical records, lab results, research, and other key documents while at the hospital treating patients. In 2013, Kraft purchased five fourth generation 16G iPads and two additional fourth generation 16G 3G-enabled iPads for librarians to use. While the staff iPads were intended to give librarians access to library resources and medical apps as they rotated to other campuses or went to conferences with less reliable Wi-Fi signals, circulating iPads have seen significantly more use than the staff iPads, possibly because library staff can do more with their desktop computers (Kraft 2015).

Kraft worked with IT personnel to make sure that the iPads were properly configured with the right software and licenses to access the hospital network. The library needed to pay a licensing fee for each device that accessed the network, as well as licenses to access the relevant resources and applications. Each device also needed a nonporous, durable outer case (to control the risk of infection) for which Kraft selected the OtterBox model and a messenger bag–style case for hands-free carrying and easy access (Kraft 2015).

Because library patrons and staff were already familiar with iPads, and some already use iPhones from the hospital as part of their work-flows, training for staff and patrons was limited to how to access the secure applications.

Hospital personnel can check out iPads for a period of up to one week. At each checkout, borrowers must read and sign the checkout agreement, including responsibility for damage. The iPads come loaded with EMR, Citrix, and a selection of library apps, including PubMed, EBSCOHost, Browzine, UpToDate, and Scopus (Kraft 2015). There is also a link to the library web page, configured to look like and be accessed as an app (Kraft 2013).

Because the usage and download of specific medical apps will vary considerably, and because new apps are being adopted at a fast pace, each borrower has the discretion to load necessary apps for the duration of the lending period. Processing a returned iPad can be a challenge, Kraft acknowledges. When the devices are returned, they need to be charged and reset. Because of the way the secure network access is configured on the device, wiping them completely is not an option, because restoring access to the network can become a problem (Kraft 2015). Instead, the devices are charged, and then a medical librarian needs to go through the iPad manually and remove all personally loaded apps, check to make sure the patron is not signed into the preloaded apps, and then erase browser history and cookies. This adds about a day of turnaround time to processing a returned iPad and getting it ready for the next patron.

The Takeaway: While the network access and privacy concerns, as well as the topical nature of the medical apps, are unique to a hospital library, a few key lessons emerge. It bears repeating that working close-ly with IT is absolutely indispensable to your device program. Remem-ber to build the cost of licenses and accessories like durable cases into the budget for each device. When purchasing devices, knowing that they will be used outside of the library's Wi-Fi network could mean that a 3G- or 4G-enabled device is a better option.

Librarians at libraries of all sizes and specialties have recognized the importance of learning from one another and sharing program ideas when launching tablet programs or any other major endeavor in the library. Let these examples of the way libraries of different sizes and specialties are using tablets, and some of the lessons they've learned, help spark some ideas and answer questions you might have about developing your own program. Chapter 6 will offer a few more tips and tricks gathered from library professionals.

5

STEP-BY-STEP LIBRARY PROJECTS FOR TABLETS AND APPS

Looking at some of the ways libraries of different types and sizes are using tablets is a great way to generate ideas for your own library's tablet program. In this chapter, you'll work through the practical steps of some sample projects. You can use these tablet projects to train your staff, to build new and better patron services, manage device programs, and publicize your tablet offerings. Although they incorporate some new skill sets and ways of thinking about information, these projects build on existing library programs and goals, like providing advisory to patrons, making presentations, and lending resources.

PROJECT 1: PLANNING FOR A SUCCESSFUL TABLET PROGRAM IN YOUR LIBRARY

Planning is the most important part of launching any tablet project. This introductory project will cover basic considerations and skills that apply to any type of tablet project, whether presentation-based or hands-on. Keeping a few basic aspects of technology setup and mainte-nance in mind will help any tablet program run smoothly, no matter its setup or audience. Then, you'll learn how to adapt your existing presen-tation skills to showcase the best tablets can offer. Finally, you'll assess where your staff is in their tablet skill set and begin thinking about ways to draw on the skills and knowledge of library volunteers to help your tablet programs be even better.

Basic Guidelines for Preparing Any Tablet Project

Whether geared for staff training or designed to enhance patron services, a few basic guidelines apply to preparing for any tablet project.

- Work with IT to be sure that all the devices involved are running smoothly. That includes the tablets themselves, along with any projection screens, and even access to the wireless network to transfer data and download or run apps.
- Make charging the devices a part of the routine. You might be surprised how quickly a live demonstration of a few different apps can drain the battery, or how long the device takes to charge back from completely drained after being borrowed.
- Remember that keeping a device clean and ready for the next patron means both restoring it to default settings and checking for physical damage and cleanliness.
- Checking the devices for condition, cleanliness, and function should be built into short-term use of the tablets within the library, as well as after extended borrowing.
- Remember to also check and maintain mounted tablets for function and cleanliness, and to reset them to defaults, in the same way.
- As stressed in previous chapters, make sure you test devices, hardware, and apps thoroughly, ideally over a period of time, before launching your tablet program. Thorough testing helps you and your staff get comfortable and fluent with what the devices are supposed to do, and with responding to unexpected glitches. There will always be glitches.

Giving a Successful Presentation Using Tablets

Whether you're training staff to use a wide variety of tablets for instruction and outreach (Projects 2 and 3), conducting an Appvisory session (Project 4), or leading an e-book-centered children's storytime (Project 6), the way you set up a live demonstration session will be similar. You'll

Figure 5.1. Giving a presentation using tablets and projection screen at the Pasadena Public Library (Image courtesy of the Pasadena Public Library)

be presenting by using one tablet connected to a large projection screen. All eyes are going to be watching how you navigate the screen. You're going to want to build some extra time to double check the physical setup of the projection screen.

Staging Your Tablet Presentation Effectively: Some Considerations

- Are there clear sight lines all around the presentation area?
- Is glare a factor?
- How much time does the screen need to warm up before the presentation?
- Any connection issues to watch for between device and projector?
- How is the wireless access and speed for multiple users accessing content on their own devices at the same time?

When it comes time to practice the presentation itself, supplement your existing presentation skills by fine-tuning the following skills for good digital presentations.

Tips for Giving an Effective Presentation Using Tablets

Speak and navigate more slowly. This will help your message stay clear and help keep your navigation from dizzying your audience following along on the projection screen.

Think in terms of elevator pitches. Whether presenting devices, appvisory, or describing the elements of a story program, prepare a few sentences of description to make the main purpose of each device or app easier to remember.

Practice your own sight lines. Transitions between looking at your device, the projection screen, and out at your audience, while remembering what you plan to say, can feel disorienting. Build in extra practice time to rehearse to help it all come together.

Step back and let your audience get hands-on. Whether it's a presentation to train staff or entertain and educate patrons, as a general rule your audience will get more out of the presentation once you step back and give them a chance to explore.

Prepare a tangible summary. Make sure that your audience has something physical as a takeaway. You'll want to give them a record of exactly which resources you used and a few of the main tips you wanted to convey, as well as links to any relevant apps or other references. Offering paper copies of a handout is one option. Archiving presentations on the web or on social media is another.

See the "After the Project" and "Taking the Project Further" sections of the projects below for ideas tailored to publicizing each of these projects and using them as tools for library outreach.

Assessing Technology Resources, Staff Knowledge, and Volunteer Resources for Your Projects

Using tablets for projects in your library relies on planning to have the access to materials, staff training, and technological support you need to get the program launched and to maintain it over time. Before undertaking any of these projects, it's a good idea to work through some of the assessments and questions outlined in more detail in chapter 2.

While the "Planning" section of each project outlined below will cover the preparation steps you'll need to take and resources you're going to need to assemble for each specific project, some factors hold true across all of them. You will want to make sure that you have adequate space to store, charge, and maintain your devices, as well as a good way to set up a space for any live demonstrations using a screen you can connect to a range of devices.

You will also need to assess how comfortable your staff is with using a range of devices, and with answering sometimes unpredictable questions from patrons about the devices used or proposed for your own library programs as well as those used by the patron population as a whole. Project 2: The Tech Petting Zoo and Project 4: Appvisory Presentation can be used as training to educate staff about a range of devices and apps at once, and can be repeated to foster ongoing and updated learning. Project 3: Using Staff Tablets for Roving Reference and Instruction is geared toward training staff to use tablets to streamline library operations and educate patrons about library resources and tablet programs.

Assessing Key Skills for Staff in a Device-Friendly Library

Beyond knowledge about a range of devices and apps, you will also want to make sure to assess staff for the following range of skills, and, depending on the structure of your library, set up one-on-one coaching or formalized group training sessions to bring them up to speed.

Presentation and Public Speaking Skills. No matter how extensive a librarian's knowledge of a range of technological devices, the ability to communicate about them clearly and engagingly is essential to making a demonstration work.

Basic Troubleshooting for Devices. No matter how carefully you plan and rehearse these, or any tablet projects you plan for your library, things will go wrong. Work with your IT department and any support team available from device or system vendors to plan for troubleshooting devices and make sure to train staff in some basic troubleshooting techniques to assist patrons in using library devices or accessing electronic resources. Make sure that training includes when and how to seek outside help in fixing the problem. When rehearsing for a live presentation, sketch out one or two backup plans or strategies in case of a glitch, like wireless not connecting or an app crashing.

Ongoing Device Use and Learning. If you have the resources, purchase enough devices to designate one for each staffer to use and load them with the same staff profile comprising both the resources available on patron tablets and apps and tools for daily work and library operations. Encourage staff to use library tablets as part of their daily workflow, such as using a tablet for reference interviews or stack maintenance tasks. Also encourage them to add a mobile app spin to their existing programming subject responsibilities, with topics like children's programming, business skills development, or social media education (Abdullah-Abouelaziz 2015; S. Taylor 2015).

Flexibility and Alternatives. Even armed with basic troubleshooting knowledge and skills, staff involved in the device program will need to be flexible enough to respond to snags and glitches effectively and calmly. Prepare some alternatives, like offering an alternate device or app if the one being sought has hit a snag. That's yet another reason to equip staff with ongoing training on multiple device platforms and apps. (See Project 2 and Project 3.)

Working with Library Volunteers

Library volunteers can be a tremendous asset to developing and running tablet projects in your library. When you train patron volunteers to assist with programs, you may find you learn even more from their help than they do from you! You may want to plan structured projects for your volunteers, but remember to be open to serendipity as well. Tech-savvy volunteers can help demonstrations and instructional programs run more smoothly by contributing ideas for apps and features to demonstrate, or being on hand to help answer questions. Patrons with technology skills to share, or experience in a specific area like coding or graphic design, can devise and lead their own demonstrations. Volunteers don't always have to take on public speaking roles. Kate Pickup-McMullin tells the story of one patron in particular, whose suggestions to create instructions for the library's downloadable e-book and audiobook service turned into her becoming the library's volunteer Apple/download library specialist (2015). Draw on patrons with special interests or perspectives—like parents, children, or entrepreneurs—to help find and test apps you're thinking of adding to the collection to help develop a collection that meets their needs. If your library already runs patron-driven advisory groups, like a teen planning committee, so much the better. Invite them to contribute ideas for apps to feature in programs.

Putting Planning into Practice for Tablet Projects

The following projects will build on the preparation and skills outlined above. Each project will begin by putting the project in the context of larger library practice. Then you will work through four sections:

1. Planning Your Project: covers the decisions you will need to make and the resources you will need to assemble before launching the project
2. Running Your Project: covers the steps of running the actual project and helps you fill in the details
3. After the Project: how to wrap up a tablet project centered on a specific demonstration event such as a Tech Petting Zoo (Project 2) or an Appvisory (Project 4) and reset any materials to their default to get ready for the next use
4. Taking the Project Further: ideas for ways to modify a project for different situations or patron populations to extend its reach and generate more interest in the program and the library as a whole

Ready to dive in? Let's get started!

PROJECT 2: DEMONSTRATING MULTIPLE DEVICES IN A TECH PETTING ZOO

No matter the purpose, platform, or number of tablets your library chooses to use in its programming, ensuring that staff is familiar with the functions and apps of a number of different devices will be an important part of your library's service. Whether asking for guidance in accessing library resources on their own devices, or seeking more general tech help with the brand-new devices they got as holiday gifts, patrons will turn to their librarians with questions about a wide range of

Figure 5.2.   Tech Petting Zoo in progress at the Southwest Harbor Library (Image courtesy of the Maine State Library)

different devices. Taking the time to educate librarians about a number of different devices helps them keep pace with patron needs, ensuring that they are able to answer questions effectively (Pickup-McMullin 2015). A good way to bring staff up to speed on a number of devices at once is to set up a Tech Petting Zoo, combining a demonstration of a range of devices at once with hands-on time to explore the devices. Librarians appreciate the staff-led program as an unbiased educational opportunity from their peers, rather than from a store or brand affiliate interested in selling a particular device (Leadbetter 2015). Showing several devices at once highlights the point that navigation and tasks are very similar across devices, and that working with them isn't as new or daunting as it seems (Pickup-McMullin 2015).

Planning Your Tech Petting Zoo

Although the opportunity to showcase a number of device types at once makes a Tech Petting Zoo a rich learning opportunity, don't feel pressure to master and present or budget for every iteration of every device platform available. The questions you asked to assess staff knowledge, tech resources, and patron interest in different types of device models (see chapter 2) can help you decide which devices to present. Present a range of types of devices to give a cross-section of the options out there. For example, assemble a selection of one or two e-readers like the Kindle Paperwhite or Nook, media readers such as the Kindle Fire and Nook HD, and a selection of tablets like the iPad, iPad Mini, Microsoft Surface, or Google Nexus. Because they represent the broadest ecosystem of apps and versatile functions, tablets are likely to generate the most interest (Leadbetter 2015). You will want to limit each Petting Zoo presentation to a total of no more than four device models, to keep things manageable in under an hour. (You can host a series of Petting Zoo presentations around different device models.)

In order to set up a Tech Petting Zoo event in your library, you will need the following basic resources:

- A space set up with a clearly visible projection screen that can connect to and mirror multiple device types for the presentation portion
- Chairs and tables where your audience has room to explore different devices freely. In order to facilitate free exploration, leaving the devices free rather than attaching them to stands or security cords is best
- Fully charged duplicates of each device you plan to present. One complete set will be for the demonstrator, and the rest will be used in turn by the audience. Note: Because of heightened interest in tablets, you may want to plan to provide three or four of each tablet device model for audience use, versus one or two of each e-reader you're presenting
- Make sure none of the devices have any restricted settings, to ensure full exploration
- A minimum of two people running the event. Plan for one presenter and at least one staff member or volunteer on hand to assist or answer questions as they occur

Running Your Tech Petting Zoo

Begin the Tech Petting Zoo with a brief introduction of each of the devices that will be demonstrated (a three- to five-minute overview of each device) followed by twenty or thirty minutes focusing on each device in turn, demonstrating one or two features or tasks, and having your audience take turns getting hands-on with the devices. The most effective way to instill confidence from the start of your Tech Petting Zoo is to remind your audience of what they already know by walking through some of the basics as a series of questions and answers. For example, Kate Pickup-McMullin, tech ninja and assistant director at the Southwest Harbor Public Library in Maine, demonstrates each device by introducing the power buttons, cord outlet, and other basic controls, before walking her audience through connecting to wireless with a series of questions inviting audience response: "Where would you look to find what you need to get connected to Wi-Fi? Answer: Settings. Question: Where in settings?" For each device, demonstrate how to connect to wireless, then pick one or two unique features to demonstrate.

Sample Topics for a Tech Petting Zoo

Here are some suggestions to get you started.

- Accessing and downloading library resources (books and other media)
- Changing settings such as volume or text appearance
- Taking pictures or screenshots
- Using sharing functions
- Demonstrate one or two tablet apps (If the tablets are part of a demonstration of multiple devices, be especially selective with apps, and save a more extensive demonstration of apps for an Appvisory.)

Open the session for questions, allowing ample time during and after the presentation. Also, collect feedback either conversationally or in written form.

The Tech Petting Zoo isn't just a terrific program for staff training; it can be a great resource for patron education as well. Depending on the structure of your library, you may find that patrons are curious enough to drop in to a Petting Zoo presentation intended for staff education. Be watchful for audience response indicating that your librarians are focusing more on patron possibilities than on the learning itself. Although the Maine Library Development Department launched its Tech Petting Zoo as a staff training initiative, Pickup-McMullin observes that many librarians focus more on the reactions of patrons to the program than on learning about the devices themselves, perhaps because delivering programs and access to patrons is such a cornerstone of their job. This division of attention is magnified by having patrons in attendance at the actual event. One solution she proposes would be to run one demonstration with librarians and volunteers and partner with them to create a presentation to the patrons at a later date (Pickup-McMullin 2015).

While the Petting Zoo demonstration familiarizes librarians with the basics of several devices at once, the best way to gain fluency with a device is to use it for daily tasks over a period of time. For busy librarians, finding time to explore a device in downtime at work can be next to impossible. One solution is to arrange for librarians to check out the devices to take home, where they could explore the device without having to balance the demands of work (Pickup-McMullin 2015). This not only gives librarians a chance to become more fluent with the uses of tablets, it can be a kind of soft launch to help you test the procedures and workflows involved in setting up a tablet lending program for patrons (see Project 5). Plan to have librarians check out devices and accessories over a period of up to a week, ideally including at least one of their days off. To help structure their exploration of the device, you may want to assign them a series of tasks.

Suggested Tasks to Teach and Master for a Tablet-Friendly Library

Some sample tasks to have them try on their own, using different devices, include

- Download an e-book using a library account and read it using a reading app.
- Take a picture and share it on social media.
- Take notes or manage a schedule using a productivity app.
- Use the QR scanner to access an enhanced shelf-talker in the library.
- Access the app version of a library database.

- Check how the library website looks and feels when using a device. (Feedback from this task will be helpful to share with IT and user experience librarians.)

Taking the Tech Petting Zoo Project Further

As noted above, extending a Tech Petting Zoo from a staff training activity to a patron education opportunity can reinforce staff knowledge as well as engage patron interest. Having recently trained staff host a Tech Petting Zoo geared toward patrons can reinforce their knowledge. A Tech Petting Zoo can also be turned into a publicity opportunity to extend the library's reach. Invite local officials, media, and educators to come to a demonstration.

Another idea, albeit one that becomes more logistically complex, is to turn the Tech Petting Zoo into a mobile enterprise. Provided your library system already has a secure and efficient infrastructure for interlibrary loan and shipping, multiple libraries in the system can share one set of Tech Petting Zoo materials. In addition to having a solid shipping system, you will need to make sure to purchase a secure case to transport the suite of Tech Petting Zoo tablets as a whole. For example, experimenting with different configurations of tethers and cages, the Maine State Library decided on the TabletShuttle Case from Explorer Cases for transit and storage, and used a locking system from Compu-Cages when needed to secure individual devices (Leadbetter 2015).

Turning the Tech Petting Zoo into a mobile enterprise between libraries also means planning for preparation for travel time for staff trainers to facilitate Tech Petting Zoo events and answer questions. Plan to have at least one facilitator and an assistant running the training, although having access to two or three assistants is an even better idea. Depending on staff knowledge and availability, you may also want to plan to recruit volunteers to assist the presentation.

PROJECT 3: USING TABLETS FOR STAFF INSTRUCTION AND ROVING REFERENCE

Whether tracking down resources to help patrons solve reference queries, or managing the many tasks and priorities that make up library management, the daily work of librarianship relies on being able to access large stores of information. In libraries of all sizes, librarians from all departments deliver service at the reference desk and the circulation desk, managing information needs and library operations from desktop computers. But, thanks to the processing power and flexibility of tablets, delivering these services no longer means having to be tethered to a central desk. Using a staff tablet loaded with key apps for library operations, sharing, and productivity, librarians can deliver important services and education from virtually anywhere in the library.

One of the most important elements of training staff to provide responsive patron service using tablet resources is to make sure they are fluent with tablet functions and a range of apps. Using tablets on a daily basis to complete work tasks and share information resources is a great way to build that fluency (Abdullah-Abouelaziz 2015; Pickup-McMullin 2015). No matter what plans you are developing to use tablets in your library, plan to designate some tablets of the same model and platform for staff-only use. Outfitting tablets with a range of information resources and productivity apps turns them into a mobile workstation, meaning that librarians can deliver patron services on the spot from anywhere in the library, or can work on library maintenance projects like shelf-reading with better information at their fingertips.

Setting up two or three tablets for staff use in roving reference (King 2015) and other library operations is a smart move when starting a new tablet program because it combines hands-on staff training opportunities with building publicity for the program as your patrons see roving librarians using tablets. Well-equipped staff tablets are also an asset to librarians who do a lot of instruction in the library and elsewhere, by helping consolidate the resources they will need to give a good instructional presentation to educate their audiences about library resources.

Planning Your Staff Tablet Project

Before using tablets for library operations and patron services, you will need to choose what platform and model of tablet will be used for the project. Ideally, this will be a model that is identical to the one being chosen for use in other library programs. (If your library program uses multiple types of tablets, work with IT and access services to determine which tablet will be the best for staff use.) Make sure the wireless signal is strong in most of the areas where staff will be using the tablet and, if necessary, work with IT to find solutions to strengthen it (a service your entire patron base will appreciate).

Load your staff tablets with a range of productivity apps, library resources, and educational resources. The staff tablets will extend what your staff can currently do on their own work computers or the ones at the reference and circulation desks, so you may want to look to those desktops for ideas of what to include, as well. Including apps and tools that are already familiar from desktop versions helps staff make the transition between using a desktop and a tablet for work tasks. You may also want to seek feedback from your more digitally savvy staff members on apps and capabilities of tablets that they would find the most useful.

Suggested Apps to Load onto Staff Tablets

- A link to the library's online catalog and website.
- Barcode scanner and QR code scanner.
- Dropbox or similar for file transfers.
- Writing program for taking notes. Ideally, use a program like Evernote or Google Docs, which can be synced to other library computers.
- Links to any subject-specific databases or apps that are used heavily.
- Social apps like Twitter and Instagram for live-tweeting responses to reference questions or other engaging behind-the-scenes content.
- A GPS-enabled app or device-tracking setting, such as Find My Phone for iOS or Android Device Manager for Google and Android devices, to help locate tablets that may have "roved" to an unknown location. (This may require enabling location tracking settings on individual devices.)
- Presentation software and graphics editing software to assist with instruction.
- If the roving librarian is conducting headcounts or tracking reference interaction, try using Suma, an open-source web and tablet tool for collecting and analyzing observational data about space, interaction, and usage developed at the North Carolina State University Library. More information can be found at http://www.lib.ncsu.edu/reports/suma.

Beyond equipping the tablets with software and apps, you will also want to outfit each staff tablet with a protective case that has pockets to keep its cords and accessories handy, and to store other spare items like pieces of paper and pens. One option is to purchase a case that's similar to the ones you're using for any tablet lending program. However, if the tablets are going to see a lot of roving use in the stacks, consider a satchel-style carrying case with a strap that can be worn across the body, to leave your staff with the option to work hands-free shelving or retrieving books, or working with patrons. If the staff tablets are going to be propped up on desks often, a case that includes a stand option is worth considering.

How you conduct training prior to the launch of your staff tablet program will depend on individual members' familiarity and ease with technology, and the size of your staff overall. You'll know whether your staff will respond best to going over the tablets in a meeting or demonstration, or by working with your staff individually to walk through specific functions, apps, and tasks staff can complete using the tablets. If staff tablets are going to be used for institutional social media accounts, it is important to clarify expectations in terms of kinds of content and photographs that would be the most helpful. Because using the tablets is both an educational opportunity and a way to provide library service, you may want to set up a schedule for the shared tablets, so that each librarian gets a chance to practice using the tablets to complete different tasks. How you set up that rotation, and whether you make the use of tablets mandatory for certain tasks, will depend on factors like your relationship with your staff and your staff's initial comfort level with the technology and apps included.

Running Your Staff Tablet Program

After some training to introduce the tablets and apps to your staff, make the tablets available for work use on a daily basis. Your staff's roles and level of comfort with the tablets, as well as patron needs, will help determine where the staff tablets see the most use. Introducing the tablets on the cusp of a large weeding project could make the tablets an asset in recording weeding data in the stacks. A librarian helping a patron might take a tablet into the stacks to help track down a resource, or to select alternatives to a book that's been checked out. Because a librarian using a tablet to do solitary work can appear unapproachable, a librarian roving the stacks to provide reference and readers' advisory might want to wear a nametag or badge that invites patrons to ask questions.

Suggested Training Tasks to Introduce Staff Tablets Gradually

If integrating tablets into daily workflows would be a significant change in practice for members of your staff, it's a good idea to introduce the tablets more slowly, and tie them to specific projects or goals. For staff members who are very new to using tablets, introduce one or two new tasks at a time and allow time for practice over a few days before introducing others.

Here are some ideas to use as a starting point for training and building confidence with tablet use:

- Take notes on a tablet during a meeting or presentation.
- Use a tablet to record information during shelf-reading or weeding of a specific section or shelf, and share documents through Evernote.
- Take pictures with a tablet during a presentation or event and share the photos on the library's social media.
- Use a tablet to access and present resources during a reference interview at the desk.
- Use a tablet to access the catalog to provide readers' advisory.
- Answer patron questions about the functions of the tablet itself (an especially useful skill to build in advance of the start of the semester or holiday gift-giving, when many patrons are likely to need overall device help).

The key to running your project for staff use tablets is to know your staff well, and to be willing to experiment. Launching staff tablet use is pretty straightforward: load them, charge them, and conduct any training needed to help staff master key library tasks. But communication is essential. Check in after the first few times of using tablets to complete tasks: How did it go? Did tablets make the workflow feel more or less efficient, after the initial learning curve? What was patron response like? Are the apps on the tablet useful, or would more, or different ones, be better?

Taking Staff Tablets Further

How far you can take the use of staff tablets in your library will depend, again, on staff comfort levels with using tablets for different tasks, as well as the workload of your library staff as a whole. How much your staff incorporates tablets into daily tasks will depend on individual projects, interest, even the time of the year. Some staff members may find the tablets more useful for unstructured exploration and work on the go, augmenting, but not replacing desktops. Some staff members learning to use tablets for the first time may be resistant initially, but after a learning curve they may be more willing to incorporate tablets into more projects, or even to propose new ones!

To help keep your staff's skills sharp over time with using tablets and apps to assist patrons, consider pairing staff use of tablets with Appvisory presentations (see Project 4) to showcase and share knowledge of new apps. Or consider making Appvisory a more collaborative process among the staff, encouraging them to share new app discoveries with one another and experiment with them on the staff tablets.

PROJECT 4: APPVISORY

Even before developing and launching your own library's tablet program, you may find that you and your colleagues are fielding questions from patrons about how to find good apps for time management, photo retouching, sharing recipes, or graphic design that are compatible with a variety of device operating systems. As seen in chapter 3, helping patrons choose and access quality apps is an extension of librarians' role as media mentors, expanding on the same critical assessment skills as traditional roles in collection development and advisory. As with other forms of advisory services, the ability to assess quality apps relies on research, seeking reviews from trusted sources, and knowing the needs and interests of different patron groups.

You'll use your ability to evaluate quality apps to help outfit tablets for individual patron use as part of your tablet lending program (see Project 5) or for mounted tablets stationed throughout the library (Project 7). You can also build on knowledge of apps to engage patron interest by creating Appvisory presentations highlighting useful and unique apps. Building Appvisory presentations and hosting them as live events in your library serves the dual purpose of showcasing the library's technological resources and the value of librarians' expertise in helping patrons make sense of the crowded landscape of available apps. Like a Tech Petting Zoo, an Appvisory presentation combines a librarian-led presentation with hands-on time to allow your audience to explore.

Planning Your Appvisory Project

Researching and assembling lists of apps to present may be the most time-consuming part of planning an Appvisory demonstration. If your library already has, or is in the process of launching, a tablet program of its own, presenting your library's first Appvisory demonstration based on the apps you already have cuts down on research and prep time, and doubles as a publicity opportunity. But figuring out what to do next can be daunting! Chapter 3 introduced the process of vetting and selecting quality apps, along with sources for recommendations and types of apps that might appeal to special populations in your library. Use the demographics and information needs of your patron population to guide topics and ideas. While each Appvisory presentation doesn't absolutely need its own self-contained theme, it absolutely does need to be structured around the general demographic groups you anticipate will attend. If you have significant patron populations like elementary school age children and parents, older adults, or teens, plan, publicize, and run Appvisory presentations targeted toward them, as well as presentations focusing on new or themed collections of apps with more general appeal.

Rather than sitting down to brainstorm a selection of apps for a specific population, or focusing on a single topic all at once off the top of your head, you may want to turn the process into an ongoing one, and jot down topic and app ideas as they catch your attention. (Having access to a tablet of your own equipped with a notes app you can sync remotely is a great asset here.)

Sample Resources for Apps and Appvisory Themes

Still feeling stuck? Here are some more ideas to guide your browsing blogs for app selections:

- **Free App Friday.** On Fridays, many app developers drop their prices or offer apps for free. This can be a collection resource, or can spark a topic or theme for your Appvisory presentation.
- **Timely Topic.** Select financial management or health apps to capitalize on New Year's resolutions in January, financial and tax apps at tax time, or back-to-school apps in late August. Or use the Fourth of July to get patriotic with American history apps.
- **Get Cooking with Apps.** Showcase some recipe sharing and discovery apps, and unify specific recipes with a theme like healthy cooking or chocolate.
- **Language and Culture.** Focus on learning languages as a whole, or build a theme around a specific country by, say, presenting an app to learn Spanish with a recipe app to find tasty paella recipes; try Prado's mobile app and your library's digital collection of Spanish language books and media, and round it out by using Google Earth to show off Spanish-speaking countries.
- **Trivia and Research.** Present a selection of apps to give patrons fast references and fun facts, not just for academics, but for friendly competition by showing off trivia apps or for solving the questions that come up over dinner: "Who did he play in that movie?"
- **Science and Technology.** From astronomy to zoology, focus on the quirky, trivia-based aspects of exploration with cutting-edge science apps to capture the interest of patrons of all ages.

Other Appvisory Selection Considerations

As you plan your topical lists of apps, and test unfamiliar ones you're considering, remember to make note of the cost and platform of each app in your themed grouping. For a great app, cost isn't necessarily a deal breaker, but it needs to be noted when it is a factor for initial or in-app purchase. In presenting Appvisory, and posting past presentations on social media, make a note of the date you determined and recorded the cost. Platform is another consideration for Appvisory selection. If your own library's resources or your patron population's interest skews heavily toward one operating system over another, you may want to focus on that platform in your presentation. Otherwise, look for apps that are compatible with multiple platforms when possible, and, if not, clearly indicate the app's operating system in both your presentation and the archived materials.

Getting Ready to Present: The Final Steps

Once you have about eight to ten apps centered on a theme, you're ready to present. No matter your topic, the basic setup and outline for your Appvisory is the same. Plan to have your selection of apps pre-loaded onto a number of fully charged tablets to use in the demonstration. Preparing copies of a paper handout with a list and description of the apps being presented, along with lists of links to download the apps and learn more, helps the presentation go smoothly, as well as providing a resource your audience can use after the presentation (Driscoll, Hurtado, and Rojo 2014).

Ideally, plan to make eight to ten devices available, and have your audience take turns. To help the sharing of devices go smoothly, make a series of numbered tickets corresponding to the number of devices you have, and start the hands-on portion of the demonstration by giving the tickets to the first group of participants, who will then hand off the devices to the next group (Driscoll, Hurtado, and Rojo 2014).

When publicizing the event, you may also want to invite attendees to bring their own devices to the presentation. If you anticipate that a number of participants will choose to do so, build in extra time for them to download the apps you've selected on the day of the event.

Running Your Appvisory Demonstration

- When setting up the event, make sure all of your devices are fully charged and activate each of the apps at the screen where you want your patrons to start exploring. (You can leave multiple apps running on your devices at once, but be mindful that this might drain the battery over the course of the presentation.)
- Begin your presentation with a short introduction to the program and its theme as a whole. Then spend a few minutes introducing each of the apps and demonstrating its functions on your projection screen.
- Encourage your audience to follow along on their paper handouts, rather than diving into the apps on their tablets as you present them.

- If your audience is taking turns with the tablets, allow ten to fifteen minutes of uninterrupted exploration with the tablets before having them switch.
- Encourage participants to save questions for the transition time between turns, to keep things running smoothly.
- Build in extra time for questions and for more free play with tablets at the end of the presentation.

After the Appvisory Demonstration

To keep the interest in these carefully curated and topically presented apps going, you'll want to make sure they stay in patrons' view. Load recommended apps onto both circulating and in-house devices. Encourage (and train) staff to call attention to apps from past Appvisory presentations when working with patrons who are using circulating or in-house tablets. Assemble handouts, presentation slides, and app lists on your library blog, or collect the list of past Appvisory topics and apps as a LibGuide. With its visual format and easy-to-use sharing functions, the social media site Pinterest can be used to maintain boards devoted to apps for different patron populations. For example, the Pasadena Library in Pasadena, California, maintains boards collecting apps for different age groups and interests, such as reading readiness and sing-along apps for preK, and age-appropriate, topical, skill-development, and learning apps for elementary school age children and teens.

Taking the Appvisory Project Further

As in Project 2, the Tech Petting Zoo, the basic Appvisory presentation can be varied to adapt to a number of different audiences. It can be used as a staff training or professional development tool. You can take the Appvisory out into the community, presenting at schools or town hall meetings as an outreach and education strategy.

Tailoring Appvisory Presentations to Specific Populations

Based on the selection of apps and a few other considerations, you can take Appvisory presentations further by tailoring them to different patron populations. Here are a few sample ways to tailor Appvisory to different audiences that can help get you started.

Library Professional Development/Staff Training Apps
- The library's own catalog, including any mobile checkout functions
- Databases and other reference resources
- Goodreads to support book clubs and reader advisory
- QR code scanner apps to assist with shelf-reading
- Apps used in the other types of Appvisory programs outlined in this section
- Participant recommendations: encourage them to demonstrate their own favorite apps or brainstorm Appvisory topics for patrons

Entrepreneurs and Small Business Owners
- Apps for document editing and management such as Google Docs, Dropbox, Evernote
- Apps for task management like Todoist, Wunderlist, or Any.do
- Financial management and e-commerce apps like Expensify or QuickBooks mobile

Elementary School Children and Their Parents
- Introduction to your library's databases in their mobile forms
- STEM-based apps like Shout Science! (iOS), DIY Nano (iOS), and SkyViewer (iOS)
- Introductory coding apps like Scratch or Hopscotch (iOS)
- Art and design apps like BookCreator and MoMA Art Lab (iOS)
- Storytelling apps like Toontastic

Teens
- Topical videos from Khan Academy, iTunesU, and TED Talks
- Productivity and time-management apps to help manage homework and activities
- Research databases available through the library and citation apps like Zotero and EasyBib
- Coding and development apps like MIT Appinventor or Codecademy

Book Groups
- Goodreads to help your book groups get social

- Reading apps for different platforms and features, especially those that allow taking and sharing notes and bookmarks
- Topical apps tied to the book of the month, like recipes, language learning, or history

Using Appvisory to Teach Larger Information Concepts

Another important way to expand on Appvisory presentations is to use the format of app presentation and instruction to teach concepts of digital literacy that extend beyond showcasing the apps themselves and their functions. As media mentors and educators, librarians are equipped to guide their patrons not only in what apps they choose, but how they use them to access and share information. With the proliferation of apps, media outlets, and other resources, and the increased ease of sharing, comes the need to think more critically about how to make informed and critical choices about evaluating and sharing information.

The Appvisory format of a librarian-led presentation that transitions into facilitated hands-on exploration can be a terrific venue for teaching larger skills of digital literacy to different populations. Beginning with a presentation of research and information resources from *Wikipedia* or apps tied to the library's licensed databases could lead to discussion and learning about critical skills in evaluating sources for validity. Using basic social media apps like Facebook, Twitter, and Instagram could teach teens about online reputation management, or entrepreneurs about brand-building and outreach. Thinking from a target population to information and skill development needs will help you come up with types of apps to present using this format, and will, hopefully, start enriching discussions for you and your patrons.

PROJECT 5: CIRCULATING TABLETS

As the information landscape becomes more digitally driven, constant connection and access to technology and data become more and more taken for granted and ingrained in the assumptions that drive everyday life. Librarians know that this is certainly not the case across every community or individual. Providing tablets for patrons to borrow and explore plays a key role in closing the gap of the digital divide. Making tablets available for library patrons to borrow can build on existing

Figure 5.3. Circulating tablet with case, cord, and guidelines (Image courtesy of Eau Claire Public Library)

circulation and access services workflows, and also builds on the core missions of the library, providing access to information resources as well as any needed instruction.

Planning to Circulate Tablets in Your Library

For the sake of this example, assume that you're creating a tablet circulation program from scratch, including planning policy, purchasing equipment, devising staff workflows, and keeping the program running. Starting a tablet circulation program requires a significant investment of time and thought as well as financial resources. Coordinating across departments in your library is absolutely essential. At the very minimum, you will need to coordinate between staff working in IT and Access Services. You will need to plan policies to determine responsibility for running the program and borrower eligibility, plan and budget for purchases of tablets and accessories, manage collection development of apps and licensing of content for the tablets, track circulation, set up a process to update and maintain your tablets, and train staff involved with any parts of the circulation and maintenance process.

Planning Policies for Your Circulating Tablet Program

Documenting staff roles, terms of circulation, and borrower eligibility clearly is an integral part of writing effective policy for your tablet circulation program. When beginning to draft policies for the program, draw on examples from other tablet lending programs, such as the ones profiled in chapter 4, or by searching the web and journal articles for examples to help develop your own customized template (Pollakoff 2015). Incorporate clear language into the policy for your tablet circulation program, assigning the roles for running and maintaining the program to specific library departments or staffing roles. The specifics will depend on how your library is organized, but some possibilities are Access Services, Circulation, IT, Emerging Technologies, and User Services. Working with staff in these departments to draft these policies and document workflows helps ensure that you've covered any concerns and maintained transparency (Small 2015). You will also want to keep updated documentation of the specific steps for circulating and maintaining your circulating tablets, both for policy purposes and to be modified for use as staff training manuals. These policy decisions can also be condensed to form the basis for a lending agreement you give patrons to sign.

Considerations for Tablet Circulation Policies

Duration of Borrowing Period. These can range from two to four hours for in-library use, to seven to fourteen days for initial lending period.

Renewal Eligibility. You will need to determine both the duration and number of renewals to allow for your program, based on anticipated interest and number of circulating devices. For example, the Queens Library system allows for an initial loan period of one month to be extended three times through renewals, for a total borrowing period of four months (Watson 2015).

Holds. Will patrons be allowed to place holds on the devices, or will devices be available on a first come, first served basis? The Queens Library and the Sussex County Library system, for example, allow holds to be placed on their devices. The Dover Town Library requires that patrons personally request tablets and the other unique devices they offer, as does the academic library at San Jose State University. Determining whether to allow holds will depend on the number of tablets available, patron interest, and staff resources to manage and oversee the holds queue.

Overdue Fines and Cutoff. Because of the expense of purchasing and maintaining tablets, these can be steeper than the fines for other overdue materials. Be sure to include language stating a specific time period cutoff, after which the device will be presumed missing and a replacement fee will be assessed, such as twenty-eight to thirty days.

Charge for Damage and Replacement. Your policy should make clear that the borrower will be held accountable for the cost of any damage incurred, and assign a specific monetary value to that damage. Assign a specific dollar amount to the cost of any accessories as well.

Many libraries of different types and sizes stipulate that only "a patron in good standing" is eligible to borrow tablets. Some criteria for a patron in good standing could be

- Established library card holder, for a time period greater than thirty days
- Town residency (public library) or student or faculty in good standing (academic)
- Valid government-issued ID
- No outstanding fines or lost materials on record
- Minimum age requirement of eighteen years old for library patrons
- Youth tablets signed out by a parent or guardian
- Signing a Patron Agreement in addition to checking out the tablet with a library card

Below is a Sample Tablet Borrowing Agreement:

Anytown Library Device Borrowing Agreement

Borrower Name (Print):_____

Current Address:_____

E-mail:_____Phone #:_____

Library Card #:_____
  Photo ID Verification (Staff Initials):_____

Rules of Use:

- Tablets are available for a maximum period of 14 days to borrowers in good standing (no outstanding fines, fees, or blocks on account) who are 18 years of age or older.
- Tablets must be returned to the circulation desk during library opening hours, to be checked in by a staff member. Tablets returned via the book drop will be assessed a fee of $20.00.
- Overdue fines will be charged in the amount of $10.00 per day.
- Borrower will be held responsible for any costs associated with replacement or repair of device and accessories, up to total replacement cost of $800.00. The library will not accept replacement devices or accessories purchased by the customer.

By signing this agreement, I understand that I am fully responsible for this borrowed device and its accompanying accessories, and for its timely return to the Staff at the Library Circulation Desk. I understand that I am responsible for any and all applicable fees and charges if the tablet is lost, stolen, or damaged, or if late fees or other fines are incurred.

I have read, understood, and agree to the rules of use in the Borrowing Agreement.

Borrower Signature:_____Date:_____
  Due Date:_____Staff Initials:_____

Purchasing Materials for Your Circulating Tablet Program

Getting ready for your circulating tablet program means making decisions about the number and type of devices you will purchase, as well as how you will store, charge, and maintain them. For tablets that are leaving the library, you will need to budget for the purchase of accessories and carrying cases that can hold tablets and accessories.

To determine the type of tablets to purchase, begin by assessing your library's current technological landscape, including existing systems, staff knowledge, and patron interest.

- What systems and hardware are you currently using for existing library workflows?
- Can the desktop systems already in your library be used to update and maintain the tablet system you're considering?
- Is the tablet system compatible with app versions of the software and databases you're currently using in the library?
- Do you have the staff knowledge to support and train patrons in different tablet platforms, or based on one platform over another?
- Does your patron community already favor one tablet platform over another in terms of existing knowledge, interest, or use in other aspects of their daily routine?

If the answers to the questions above could apply to multiple tablet systems or models, narrow the choices by using factors such as cost, processing power, battery life, and reviews of durability and ease of use to help make the decision. Bear in mind that these tablets are going to see heavy, unsupervised use. If tablets at different price points can offer the same capabilities, choose the more durable one or the one at a lower cost, even if it might not be the latest model. Another avenue to explore in consultation with your IT department is the purchase of refurbished tablets from a reputable source.

And remember: these questions and decisions are not intended to lock you into one tablet system and model forever. After launching your initial program, it is important to assess circulation statistics and patron needs and interest, and to stay aware of developments in new technology, to evaluate whether to add new tablet systems and models to the program. If needed, you can revisit the questions above as you plan to add more tablets at a later date.

Now that you know what type of tablets you will be circulating, the next decision to make is how many to purchase. Of course, cost and budget will be a factor in determining the number of tablets to purchase. Don't forget to factor software licenses into your purchase costs. Depending on the vendor agreement, you may need to factor in the purchase of individual licenses for the software loaded onto each tablet. However, it is even more important to use your available storage space as a guide. How big is the space set aside for the cabinet or storage cart you've designated or purchased for circulating tablets? How many devices can fit in the storage space you've allotted? How many tablets can you update, or charge, at once? Adding more tablets to a program with ample storage space ready to receive them is easier and more cost-effective than having to come up with additional secure storage space for an overly ambitious tablet purchase.

No matter the size of your library system or available budget resources, start small with your initial purchase of circulating tablets. Absolutely do not max out your storage space or budget with your initial purchase. Starting small keeps your program more flexible and easier to manage and allows you to work through any unexpected problems that will arise as you launch the circulation program. Planning the initial purchase to stay under budget is a good strategic move to get management approval for a proposed program. It also helps plan for repair and replacement costs from the start. Starting small, of course, scales to different numbers for different libraries and library systems, as does determining when to increase the number of circulating tablets. For a library that serves an entire town or academic community from one location, a purchase of five to ten tablets might make sense. For a library system piloting a program that will extend across several branches, one tablet per branch, or twenty-five tablets to share system-wide might be the number for a pilot program. Whatever the scale of your library and community, start as small as possible to work the kinks out of a pilot program.

Setting Up Workflows to Manage Your Tablet Program

After determining the number and type of tablets to purchase, the next step will be beginning to set up the configuration for the circulating tablets. A word on timing: you can begin to work on this step before having your pilot tablets in hand. The bare minimum you need is a workflow to restore your circulating tablets' device settings. Depending on the particulars of your device platform and other choices you've made about multiple device maintenance, you can restore the backed up patron profile from a cloud backup or by syncing it manually to a computer. While waiting for tablets to arrive, you can also prepare an account with the app store for your chosen platform, for example, the VPP (Volume Purchase Program) in the Apple store for iPads or Google Play for Education on Android tablets. Remember to evaluate options for bulk purchases, whether as an education entity or nonprofit: different categorizations as businesses or educational institutions apply to public and academic libraries in different app stores.

No matter what choices you've made about platforms and models of tablets, the basic workflow for maintaining the tablets will be to reset them to a default patron profile backup before lending to the next patron. Wiping the tablet completely to factory settings before restoring the default profile between borrowers is an extra step that can help preserve patron anonymity, but taking this step will depend on how IT has configured tablets.

Using a Patron Profile to Provide a Standardized User Experience

Setting a default patron profile gives your patron base equal access to the suite of circulating tablet resources. You can use the Patron profile you've configured to synchronize all your circulating tablets and restore the default settings. At its most basic, the Patron profile should include the following content:

- A link to the library catalog to search for library content.
- App versions of database resources available through your library.
- App versions of any programs needed to access downloaded library content, such as Adobe Reader, OverDrive, and Axis 360.
- Any apps you are making available to patrons on circulating tablets—either free or purchased under license through the library account. (For more on selecting apps, see chapter 3.)

If you are circulating tablets in both an adult program and a children's program, ensure that the apps selected represent a wide range of age groups and interests, by including child-friendly apps and research resources as well as links to the catalog and any apps needed to use downloaded library content. Alternately, you may want to plan to set up separate default profiles for Adult Patron and Child Patron, and may want to create multiple tiers of profiles for different children's age groups, to ensure that the selection of apps is age appropriate and aligned with their skills and interests. The librarians working directly with different age groups in the children's library can be great resources to help develop this aspect of the program. (For more interactive ways to use tablets with children's programs, see Project 6.)

Security Considerations for Circulating Tablets

Once you've worked through the process of deciding what content should be on the tablet you're going to lend, you will want to address how the library-provided content and configurations are secured. Make sure that all administrator accounts, such as the app store, are protected with secure passwords and also logged out before lending a tablet. You may choose to use security settings to limit how much patrons can alter the content on the tablets, such as downloading apps from their own personal accounts. If the tablet is loaded with a significant proportion of specialized content and configurations, such as vendor-licensed apps, you may also want to configure the devices so that nothing can be deleted without an access code (Kraft 2015). Because the general population, such as public library patrons or students, are likely to want to customize their borrowed tablets with new apps, or even to see the library's security settings as a challenge to be worked around, opt to give the circulating tablets the minimum necessary security, and to make deleting unwanted apps and patron data a part of the check-in workflow.

Managing and Resetting Device Configurations between Patrons

You have a few different options for how to set tablets to the default patron profile, depending on the tablet platform or other resources. You can treat circulating devices individually, resetting each to the backup Patron profile wirelessly, or by connecting to a desktop via USB. (Google Nexus tablets also offer the option to reset borrowed tablets by physically touching the back of the device to a device designated as the main default device.)

Multiple device management (MDM) software streamlines the management of multiple devices, allowing for wireless control of settings and permissions for a suite of different devices at once. For iPads, Apple Configurator is a free program that can be used to manage multiple devices, including the option of synchronizing them to one Patron profile.

For libraries with limited time or in-house tech resources and expertise or those planning to launch and manage many devices at once, it can be worthwhile to make a financial investment to contract with a service that can manage and update devices remotely. The tablet circulation, charging, and storage process can be automated by using a vendor kiosk that provides access and self-checkout of tablets. For example, for a library system considering iPad management, MediaSurfer by TechLogic is a self-service kiosk patrons can use to check out iPads. The kiosk charges and updates the tablets without involving staff time.

Cataloging Circulating Tablets

Preparing to integrate devices into your existing cataloging system is also an important step to take in preparing the workflow to launch the program. You will need to work closely with your library's Technical Services, Access Services, and Cataloging staff to plan how the devices will be cataloged, tracked, and checked out to patrons. Some integrated library management systems have an option to catalog and categorize the device as an "iPad," or "tablet," while other systems mean you need to get more creative. For example, because the Dover Town Library lends devices as part of a diverse system incorporating many different kinds of tech and household hardware items, they use BiblioBoard to allow patrons to discover the unique items available for circulation. Assign each device a unique name and number like "iPad1" or "Tablet3," and either have that number etched onto the device itself (a feature available for iPads) or affix a label to the device manually. Ideally, add a notation of the device's accessories to its catalog record and, if your system allows, barcode each piece, such as the charging cord, USB cables, and headphones individually, so that they can each be scanned separately when being checked in and out. This may seem like a more involved process than the typical cataloging endeavor, but it helps protect the investment you have made in your circulating tablets.

Now that your program policies are planned, your staff is trained, devices and accessories purchased and cataloged, and storage secured, you're ready to get the program running.

Running Your Circulating Device Program

No matter what choices you make for policy, device platform, lending term, default patron settings, and device maintenance workflows, if you're managing the circulation program in-house rather than through a vendor kiosk, the process will follow these steps, from initial borrowing to return.

1. Ensure that the tablet to be borrowed is fully charged and complete with all accessories, case, and carrying container.
2. Make sure borrower meets borrowing criteria and understands and signs borrowing agreement.
3. Check out tablet and accessories to patron, scanning the barcode for each item.
4. When item is returned, have a librarian manually check the device's condition. Ideally, assess the device's physical condition when the borrowing patron is present, and check to make sure that the device hasn't been locked with a passcode, because tracking down a borrower to unlock a device after the fact can be cumbersome (Woodbury 2015). Record any damage to the device or accessories.
5. Clean the physical device and accessories with disinfectant wipes to remove smudges and germs.
6. Charge the device and manually check the returned device to make sure that any added apps and patron data are deleted, along with following the general procedure to restore the device to default patron backup profile. You may want to consider wiping the device back to factory default settings before reloading the default patron profile you've set up, particularly if individual users have unrestricted access to add their own apps during the borrowing period. Return the device to storage or record and request any needed repairs.

Below is a Sample Tablet Circulation Checklist:

Anytown Library Device Circulation Checklist

Borrower Name (Print):_____

Library Card #:_____

Device Due Date:_____ Return Date:_____

Late Fines:_____

Device Physical Condition (Circle One):

Satisfactory
or
Problem Observed

Accessories Returned in Satisfactory Condition:

- Adapter
- Protective Case
- Lightning Cable
- Headphones
- Instructions

Device Checked:

- Screen in Satisfactory Condition
- Screen and Device Sanitized
- Device Activation Successful (no passcode)
- Device Restored to Default Backup Settings and Apps
- Device Checked Manually to Remove Patron Data/Apps
- Device Charged/Stored

Issues/Repairs Reported:

Date:_____Staff Initials:_____

As you can see, running and managing a device program can be time- and attention-consuming. Taking the extra steps of assessing the borrowed device manually is especially time-consuming. While different privacy configurations and safeguards on circulating devices can limit patron access to a degree, patrons will often try to circumvent those settings and add their own content or apps, leaving their data mark on the device (Farid 2015). Taking the time to delete patron data manually ensures the protection of patron privacy, especially in cases where the device configuration and permission makes resetting it to factory settings prohibitive (Kraft 2015). Staff training is absolutely essential to making sure that the device circulation program moves smoothly through these steps, especially on the return end, where potential patron data comes into play.

Tracking and Evaluating Your Circulating Device Program Over Time

In addition to managing the workflows associated with circulating individual tablets to patrons, tracking the program as it evolves over time is vital to the success of your circulating tablet program. Be prepared for high interest and heavy circulation of tablets when you first roll out the program, even in a scaled-down pilot program. With just a few signs and announcements, the novelty of the program will attract borrowers. Borrowing rates may level off in a few weeks or months, after the novelty has worn off, and different patterns of use or borrowing may emerge.

Evaluating Your Circulating Tablet Program: Start to Six Months

Tracking holds, circulation statistics, borrowing patterns, and patron feedback will help you refine your program as you manage it on an ongoing basis. Tracking circulation statistics and holds helps you make decisions about the borrowing period. Often, libraries that offer hourly borrowing or in-library circulation programs as well as longer borrowing periods find that loan periods of a week or more, and the ability to take the tablet out of the library, are significantly more popular, resulting in the decision to transfer in-library tablets to extended borrowing periods. Statistics on renewals and overdue fines can help you determine if your borrowing period needs to be extended. Tracking circulation statistics over time, and checking them against your holds queue (if your library allows holds on devices), helps inform the decision to purchase more devices or devices of different types. Because your program has, ideally, started with a pilot program of a smaller number of devices and come in under its total budget, you'll have the resources to purchase and circulate a few more tablets early on, to meet patron demand. However, because novelty is a factor in patron demand for devices, delay the decision to purchase more devices at least a month, barring significant patron demand.

Recording damage to the device and accessories will guide both immediate and longer-term purchasing decisions of both devices and accessories. Especially for tablets geared toward the youngest patrons, durability of the devices and accessories may immediately be put to the test. While you'll be evaluating wear and tear more closely at the six-month mark and beyond, especially as your devices phase out of warranty, collate any reports of loss or damage from the start of the program onward, to watch for trends like missing screen protectors or fraying headphones, indicating the need for replacing immediately with sturdier models.

Evaluating Your Circulating Tablet Program: Three to Six Months and Beyond

After your circulating tablet program has been running for a few months, logistics and policies will be refined, and practice will make workflows more efficient. Once you're past the initial novelty phase, you'll have clearer data to guide tablet settings as well as purchasing decisions.

Monitor the holds queue over time, not just for number of holds, but for repeat borrowers. Novelty will likely drive the holds queue higher in the first one to three months, and then level off over time. You'll also want to monitor the names on the holds list, not just the overall numbers. Over time, you may see a significant number of patron names repeating to fill out the holds list (Miller 2015). Keep that in mind when deciding how many devices to add to the program going forward.

You'll start to see wear and tear on devices that have been circulating over several months. Having tracked any damage to the tablets on an ongoing basis, you may see trends that guide you toward the purchase of more, or sturdier replacement accessories, or show that one device model is holding up better than another in the children's program, for example. Take a look at the software side as well, to see if you need to refine security settings on the tablets, or purchase new apps to meet patron needs.

For a program circulating several types of devices, the circulation and holds queue data can guide the decision of the number and type of devices to purchase to update the program. For example, at the Dr. Martin Luther King Jr. Library at San Jose State University, a busy academic library, IT manager Farrukh Farid, notes that students intent on doing work will choose even an older laptop over an iPad, and that the circulation of iPads has been languishing behind the other devices on offer, which is leading to a decision to phase out the iPads over time, and possibly replace them with Chromebooks or Android tablets (Farid 2015).

As you can see, managing a device program requires a significant amount of preparation, ongoing maintenance, and evaluation over time. But when it all comes together, you've given your patrons access to a valuable set of resources to increase access to library materials and opportunities to build digital literacy.

PROJECT 6: USING TABLETS IN CHILDREN'S PROGRAMMING

Crafting engaging live programs in the library has long been a cornerstone of children's librarianship. Events like storytimes draw children and their caregivers to the library, building connections and friendships in the community, and showcasing both the library's resources and librarians' roles as educators and media mentors. Integrating tablets into children's programming can enhance traditional children's programming with multimedia, while also presenting an opportunity to offer guidance to parents about best practices for using tablets to support children's digital literacy, imagination, and education.

Although there are a wealth of quality educational apps and storybooks available for different tablet programs, the use of screens and digital media by young children has been a matter of some concern for parents and educators. Plan programs for children no younger than two years old, in order to adhere to guidelines for young children's screen usage and digital consumption, which advise limiting screen and mobile time for children aged two and under (American Academy of Pediatrics Council on Communications and Media 2011).

To illustrate the ways to tailor tablet uses to children's programming most effectively, a walkthrough of the steps of creating a children's storytime event using tablets, e-books, and apps is given below. These logistics, resources, and considerations can be adapted to other uses for tablets in creating children's programming in your library.

Planning to Use Tablets in Children's Storytime

The easiest way to begin using tablets in children's programming is to build on library programs that are already in place. A great place to start is by incorporating tablets and apps into storytime in your library, creating a multimedia e-storytime event that showcases the ways tablet technology can enrich the fun and learning of a traditional storytime event. When planning e-storytime and other live children's programming, work closely with children's librarians, drawing on their knowledge of the different age groups in the children's programs, the times and days most likely to be popular and well-attended, and themes likely to be particularly well received. If possible, schedule the first e-book storytime for a space and time already established with a well-attended event, and tailor your presentation to that audience.

You will need to consider the space for staging your e-book storytime well in advance of your first planned event, to allow time for rearranging equipment and rehearsing in the designated space. Setting up the space to accommodate the technical requirements of your e-storytime is especially important if you are building on an existing time and space for a traditional storytime program. You will need to decide whether to use an already designated storytime space, or move to a different space in the library. That decision will depend on the typical size of your storytime attendance. For a smaller program that uses a cozy setup for just a handful of eight to ten children and possibly their caregivers, you can probably use an individual tablet just as you would a traditional print book, reading and showing the screen around as you go. In this single-tablet read-aloud setup, you especially need to make sure that glare is not an impediment from any angle or level of the space where people will be sitting.

If you are planning a storytime for a larger audience or a space where glare on a single tablet would be an impediment, linking the tablet to a projection screen is the way to go. You will need to make sure that you can project images from a tablet onto a larger screen, and that all the sight lines in the space will be clear, unobstructed, and glare-free for patrons of different heights. Possibilities to explore include a Smart Board, an Apple TV screen, or a computer monitor. One potential advantage of connecting to a larger screen or using other peripherals is the ability to play the sounds or multimedia, enhancing your presentation with better quality. The specifics will depend on your room setup and your library's resources. Be creative with arranging the space. If the usual storytime arrangement puts the librarian and the program focus in a narrow corner rather than a nice, flat wall for a good projection, reorienting to face a wider wall might fix the problem.

The space and technical needs might mean moving the storytime out of its customary space and into a better-equipped part of your library, like a community meeting room. Using an unaccustomed room for a children's event will mean advance planning, such as making announcements and signs of the change of venue, and moving furniture around. Make sure there is adequate seating, whether on chairs or on mats or rugs on the floor.

Once you know your physical and technical setup for the e-book storytime, it's time to get to the fun part: planning the programming. Selecting an engaging book is just one part of the program. You can build in songs, games, and even Appvisory, with the book as a centerpiece to showcase the best features of the book and the tablet technology. The children's librarians at the Pasadena Public Library integrated e-books into a storytime for preschool students that could serve as an excellent model for your own storytime program or a guide for great ideas.

A Sample Storytime Program Using Tablets

(Adapted with guidance from Jennifer Driscoll and Annmarie Hurtado, children's librarians at the Pasadena Public Library.)

1. Introduction: a welcome song, letting audience follow along using lyrics projected in the Keynote app.
2. Reading aloud from a book app.

3. Movement activity, whether instructor-led or in time with a song played through the iPad.

4. Reading from a print book on the storytime theme, which is a nice way to emphasize the connection between quality tablet resources and traditional library resources.

5. Felt board activity. Here you have the option to use a traditional, physical felt board activity, or make it tablet-based by using the Felt Board app (an interactive iOS app designed for parents and caregivers, to invite interactive play, sold for $2.99 in the App Store). A free version of the app, Mother Goose on the Loose, turns nursery rhymes into interactive exploration and sing-alongs.

6. Another book app.

7. Closing song, with lyrics projected in Keynote.

8. Handouts and resources for parents, highlighting where to find the apps and books used (Driscoll, Hurtado, and Rojo 2014).

The formula the Pasadena Public Library uses is exemplary because it combines traditional books and storytime activities with quality e-books and apps. Building a program that includes print books and physical activity as well as tablet-driven activities places the digital tools in their broader learning context. This helps make the point that carefully chosen digital media has its value in early childhood education and library programming, and that librarians can help parents make those choices.

Building on the formula of introductory song, followed by alternating between digital books and traditional books, and physical movement offers options as numerous as the array of quality children's books and possibilities for songs and apps out there. Looking at your library's own collection of digital picture books is a smart place to begin looking for a theme, because it is cost-effective and also offers a way to promote existing library resources in a new context to your audience. Or use an app or a song, or even a movement activity, to inspire a storytime theme and assemble a collection of physical and e-books around it. If your library doesn't have the e-books you're seeking, there's always the option to coordinate with the collection development librarian to enhance the library's collection in the service of your storytime. The following is a brief list of web resources you can consult for ideas to shape your storytime program and inspire themes:

- Little eLit (http://littleelit.com/) is a network of children's librarians sharing terrific resources, ideas, and app recommendations.
- The Pasadena Public Library curates its app and book recommendations into topical boards on Pinterest, including app recommendations for preschool, ages two to five (https://www.pinterest.com/pasadenalibrary/apps-we-recommend-preschool-ages-2-5/) and Staff Picks, Children's Edition of quality books for children and tweens (https://www.pinterest.com/pasadenalibrary/staff-picks-childrens-edition/).
- Digital Storytime (http://digital-storytime.com/) reviews picture book apps; access through website or app.
- International Children's Book Library (http://en.childrenslibrary.org/). Free e-books for children, from all over the world. Great multicultural resource.
- TumbleBook Library (http://www.tumblebooklibrary.com/subscribe.aspx). A subscription service your library can use to access interactive children's books for programs and e-lending.

Because an e-book storytime involves integrating technological and traditional media to present a hopefully seamless whole, finding the time to rehearse and iron out any glitches is important. Any children's librarian has the flexibility to respond to a sometimes unpredictable level of audience enthusiasm. Once technology enters the mix, that's even truer. After assembling your books and apps, do a run-through to test your technological setup and apps for any glitches, make sure the sight lines and media volumes are good, and, of course, get accustomed to the physical timing of presenting from a tablet to an audience. Have a colleague help you check your sight lines, media volume, and timing, to help make sure your e-storytime will go smoothly.

Running Your e-Book Storytime

The planning and rehearsing you've done before your first e-book storytime will mean that you're well-prepared for its debut. Whether it's going to take over or complement an existing children's storytime, be sure to advertise the e-book storytime using tablets a week or two in advance of your launch. This will help generate interest, and also give parents concerned about their children's screen use a chance to opt out.

Begin each e-book storytime by making it clear that digital screen resources will be used and displayed, to make sure parents are aware of having that option. In addition to preparing the e-books, apps, and activities you're working with, be ready with answers, and possibly a few copies of an informational handout, about what makes smart use of educational technology for young kids, because parents may ask.

No matter how prepared you feel, or how many storytimes you've run so far, plan to take a few extra minutes to set up before your storytime, queue up any apps you'll be using, and make sure that any tech is in good working order. If you're using the volume function on any devices or apps, test the levels before you get started. Then, take a deep breath, smile, and have fun entertaining and educating kids.

After Your e-Book Storytime

After you've worked through the logistics and technological considerations that go into staging your first e-book storytime event, planning and running repeat events will get easier. You can use the same spatial and technological setup to present storytimes with different themes—tied to seasons and events of the year or around new books and apps that catch your attention—or play with other ideas. Depending on how your storytime is attended and how your audience responds, you may want to shift the order of some of the elements. Change up the order and proportion of e-books to print books, add more movement and songs, or lead an in-person activity inspired by one of the books you've selected for the week. For new ideas keep checking the resources listed above, as well as drawing on the new children's books in your library.

Taking the Project Further

Working with children's tablet programming such as e-book storytime in your library can be complementary to your library's other tablet programs, including the projects outlined in this book. Using tablets in live children's programs such as an e-book storytime draws on digital presentation skills that carry over across other presentation projects using tablets. Specialized knowledge of children's programming and age-appropriate goals and resources can also help adapt some of the other projects detailed here, such as Appvisory programs, circulating tablets, or mounted tablets in the library, to be age-appropriate educational programming complementary to live e-book storytime presentations. Make information about other children's tablet programming part of the concluding announcements that wrap up your e-book storytime, and make sure circulating tablets complement storytime by providing access to the books and apps showcased during presentations.

Appvisory presentations and e-book storytime complement one another especially well. A brief walkthrough of the different apps used during the e-storytime works like a mini-Appvisory. You can also build a more focal app presentation into the storytime itself, if you have an age-appropriate interactive app that can be used to fit the theme. Apps that emphasize interaction, with questions to be answered, or with music that gets participants up and moving, are likely to work best for app presentations tied to storytime. Spare copies of handouts from Appvisory events, with age-appropriate app lists and information about the Appvisory program schedule, can capitalize on one program to build attendance at another. If your library is setting up tablets for in-library use (see Project 7), make sure the ones in the children's department are outfitted and updated to include e-books and apps featured in storytimes.

Parents and caregivers may approach librarians with questions or concerns about screen time, digital literacy, and their children's development, prompted by e-book storytime or more general concerns. An Appvisory or mini-Appvisory used in conjunction with an e-book storytime can be a great venue to allay those concerns. Librarians presenting programs for parents of young children can work from the American Academy of Pediatrics' guidelines of discouraging media use in children younger than two years of age, and use their position as media mentors to advocate enriching, interactive, and developmentally appropriate tablet uses that emphasize children's learning and exploration under a caregiver's guidance.

Another way to take the e-book storytime project further is to present the program in another venue, such as a local school or parents' group at a local community center. Partnering with other organizations provides a valuable educational opportunity, as well as an opportunity to do outreach by concluding a presentation with a mention of the program already running at the library.

If you want to take children's programming with tablets further still, you can move away from the content-driven apps like e-books and Felt Board, to use more creative tablet tools to enhance content for your presentation, or make a brand-new presentation. Options using graphic software and multimedia are limited only by your imagination and willingness to tinker with tech. Using your tablet's camera and some basic presentation software, you could create a story that uses familiar faces and places from your community. Exploring reviews of children's apps and e-books to plan your own storytimes, as in the short list of web resources above, will also show you some of the ways other libraries are using tablets and apps to build better storytimes. As you grow more accustomed to using children's e-books and apps, and the other tools and apps your tablet platform has to offer, you'll come up with creative ideas of your own to share with colleagues at your library and beyond.

PROJECT 7: USING TABLETS TO PROVIDE AND GATHER INFORMATION IN YOUR LIBRARY

In addition to the direct service interactions that place information and resources in the hands of patrons, a library facilitates information exchange more passively. At times, patrons prefer to manage their search for information on their own, from searching the library's catalog and electronic resources, to browsing the shelves in general or conducting specific searches for what they need. Rather than interacting with a librarian for every information need, they let the library speak for itself, exploring library resources in a self-guided way. Mounted tablets, configured to offer inviting displays of library content and resources, capitalize on self-directed information-seeking.

Using surveys to gather patron feedback about library service and experiences has long been a part of library practice, helping shape programs and plan new initiatives so that library services adequately represent patron needs. In order to preserve the privacy of patron data, these surveys and patron feedback should be conducted anonymously. Setting up mounted tablets designed for free, self-guided patron use creates another collection point for gathering patron use statistics. Data can be gathered in one of two ways: explicitly through surveys asking direct questions to elicit feedback about library services, or by gathering statis-

Figure 5.4. Wall-mounted tablets at the Dover Town Library (Image courtesy of Dover Town Library)

tical data about clicks and downloads, easily available from some programs and apps. Tablets set up on stands are ideally suited for these programs.

This project will cover setting up tablet stands as kiosks for both the purpose of providing and collecting patron data.

Planning to Use Mounted Tablets to Collect and Provide Patron Data

No matter how you intend to use your mounted tablets in the library, you will have to decide what model and tablet to use. The model and operating system you select for these mounted tablets will depend on the features, functions, and costs that are most important to you as well as how the tablets integrate into your library system as a whole, both in terms of staff expertise and technological compatibility. Unless cost, features, or functions make a compelling case for a particular model, plan to purchase and outfit the same model of tablet that you are already using or planning to use for other programs in your library. Because mounted tablets can showcase content and features available on tablets being used for other programs and projects, it is worthwhile to consider purchasing additional tablets to be configured as mounted tablets and accounting for any additional app and software licenses when budgeting for tablet purchases to launch another type of tablet project in your library, even if mounted tablets are not confirmed as an impending project.

For any hardware, you will want to consider cost, ease of installation, and durability, and will want to find a way to get a hands-on demonstration of the stand prior to committing to purchase, if possible. Remember that price can vary significantly between brands that are otherwise nearly identical in specifications or even between the same brand and model across different retailers. If you have the organizational freedom to pick your vendor, research prices across library-related vendors as well as retailers that sell and market to education and business. Aim to select hardware that has some cross-compatibility between different device platforms and models, so that your hardware purchase can serve your device program in the long term, adapting to upgrades or new decisions and models. A few centimeters of thickness or height can make a difference between generations of devices, and you want to be sure any hardware purchase is built to last through upgrades and replacements.

Questions to Ask When Positioning Mounted Tablets

How you intend the mounted tablets to be used will be a determining factor in where they are placed, and how they will be mounted. As you develop your plan for using mounted tablets in the library, consider the following questions.

What are patrons' sight lines? When mounting tablets on walls or stands, make sure that they are at a median eye level, and don't forget to consider accessibility for patrons who use wheelchairs.

Can you capitalize on unused space? A tablet on a stand can be a way to occupy a few feet of space near shelves. That can be a useful spot to position a tablet configured to display e-book offerings. Think of the uses of wall space as well, as possible places for mounting one or two tablets.

What are the patterns of traffic in your library? Putting a tablet kiosk near the reference or circulation desk could capitalize on traffic already directed toward it, but it runs the risk of holding up a line at a high-traffic time in the library.

How will traffic move to and around the tablets? When determining the positioning and space needs for your tablets, factor in the space the hardware and tablets will occupy, and also factor in the space needed for a person using the tablet. Make sure there are still a few feet of free space for other patrons to move around them and access resources.

Are the tablets intended to complement content or programs? If yes, make sure the stands are positioned near the relevant shelves or event spaces. Configure a tablet to display a selection of e-books near a fiction shelf, or a tablet at or near children's eye level adjacent to the space for children's programs. The Dover Town Library uses this strategy to draw relationships between the content available in its physical and electronic collection.

Are the tablets for browsing, searching, or app demonstration? Knowing how the mounted tablets are likely to be used will help you determine the best placement and type of display. Tablets intended for brief use in browsing or looking up an item or two in the catalog can be mounted on stands or walls, to be used by patrons on their way to another part of the stacks. Tablets intended for lengthier exploration of apps might be better served by mounting on a table space or tethered to a stand near a comfortable chair.

Once you have some details sketched out for how the tablets will be used, you will need to choose the way they will be mounted and secured. Tablets can be mounted on stands of varying heights, affixed to wall mounts, or secured to mounts on top of tables or even on shelves.

Types of Tablet Mounting Configurations

Here is a rundown of the general types of mounting options available.

Floor Stands: These free-standing floor stands have a base of a few feet wide and hold the tablet in a secure stand with its screen accessible to users. Some have a base of tripod legs, and others have a solid base.

Considerations: Stability and adjustability are going to be the major considerations with this kind of stand. Can the height and angle of

Figure 5.5. Tablet on a stand at the Dover Town Library (Image courtesy of Dover Town Library)

display be adjusted? What is the total area occupied by the base and stand? How is the charging cord secured?

Wall Mounts: These mounts affix the device to a wall, either flush with the wall, or using an arm, at an angle.

Considerations: Visibility of tablet screen and sight lines, as well as adjustability. Ease of mounting the tablet into the wall stand and taking it back out. (You want to strike a balance between secure and cumbersome to remove when support or modification are needed.) Think about the placement of charging cords, and stability.

Table Mounts (Solid): These metal or plastic stands have bases of different dimensions. Some clamp onto the edge of a table, while others screw into it. Security of the base to the table surface varies, as does the level of security in the way the device is held. Some can be locked in place with a key or other locking mechanism, while others rely on the structure of the mount itself.

Considerations: Security of the tablet in the base, placement of the charging cords. Design of edges and corners, especially for tablets designated for children. Amount of table space occupied. Will affixing the mount to the table surface mean drilling holes for the hardware or to accommodate the cord? How will tablet use impact other uses for the table?

Table Mounts (Tethered): These mounts use a sturdy, flexible cord and locking mechanism to fix the tablet in a protective case to a base, but allow a more free range of motion around the radius of the tablet.

Considerations: This configuration offers a more free range of motion than the others, and is ideal for tablets that are going to be used in multiple directions or angles. This is a good set up for tablets that are going to be used for sustained activity, like app browsing, reading, or program-driven exploration. It also helps secure the tablet without monopolizing a great deal of table space, which can be important if space is at a premium. If the tablets are locked into their tether with a key mechanism, make sure you have extra copies of the key stored safely in a staff area.

Kitchen Mounts: Designed to secure tablets being used to look up recipes or media in a cooking or family entertainment setting, kitchen mounts can be wall mounts or stands, or in some cases, adjustable as both. The tablet can be mounted at an angle in a small easel-type stand or mount, clamped to the counter, or affixed to a short, adjustable arm that can function as a countertop stand or mount.

Considerations: These stands' design for easy countertop or cabinet use and viewing means they are at a good angle for mounting on table-tops or for wall or shelf mounting. Because kitchen stands are designed for personal household use rather than institutional use, they may be easier to install and to swap tablets in and out. Some models may be more affordable than their institutional equivalents. However, because these stands are for household use, the tablets will not be well-secured in their stands and an additional locking mechanism may need to be purchased for security.

Configuring Your Mounted Tablet Display

Configuring your mounted tablets into kiosk mode allows you to determine what apps and functions browsing patrons will be able to use. You can use kiosk mode to lock the tablet into a specific app or set of apps, to focus on the desired content experience.

Configuring Android Tablets in Kiosk Mode

Locking an Android tablet into kiosk mode requires the download of a dedicated app. There are numerous options available in the Google Play store. Options include SureLock, Kioware, and Kiosk Browser Lockdown. Work with IT to choose and install the most appropriate one.

Configuring iPads in Kiosk Mode

On iPads, enable kiosk mode by setting up Guided Access using the following steps (Apple 2015):

1. From Settings go to General Accessibility, then choose Guided Access.
2. Turn Guided Access on and set a Passcode to control Guided Access, in order to prevent users from leaving an active session. Remember to record this passcode somewhere secure for staff use.
3. In Settings for Guided Access, turn off the Motion setting to prevent switching the device from portrait to landscape orientation.

4. To disable parts of the screen during the Guided Access session, trace a circle around any areas of the screen you want to disable during Guided Access and use the handle icons to adjust the area.
5. To start a Guided Access session around a specific app (such as your online catalog or a menu of e-resources), triple-click the Home button, then set up the app or apps you want to run and adjust any settings for the app.
6. Click Start to begin the session.
7. To end the session, triple-click the Home button and enter the passcode.

Configuring Microsoft Surface Tablets in Kiosk Mode

Setting up Assigned Access on a Microsoft Surface tablet lets you lock it to a specific Windows application for use as a mounted tablet kiosk. There are two parts to the process.

First, you will need to create a Local Account on the Surface tablet (Rathbone 2014).

1. Swipe from the right side to access the Charms bar, and tap Settings.
2. Tap the Change PC Settings link.
3. Tap Accounts (left column) to bring up the Users section.
4. Tap Other Accounts (left column) and then tap Add a User.
5. Tap Sign In Without a Microsoft Account.
6. Create the New User Account with the Username "Kiosk" and a Password.

Next, you will use the Local Account configuration to configure settings for the kiosk.

1. Log into the Local Account and set the website or app display you want.
2. Log out, then log back in using the Administrator Account.
3. Swipe from the right to pull up the Charms bar, then tap Settings.
4. Tap Change PC Settings.
5. On the Settings Screen, select Accounts, then select Other Accounts.

6. Below the list of accounts (you should see the Kiosk account you set up in the prior instructions), you will see "Set up account for Assigned Access." Click on it.
7. Click on Choose an Account, and choose the Kiosk account you set up.
8. On the same screen, click Choose an App.
9. Exit by pressing the Surface button on the tablet, swiping down or tapping the arrow in the upper left corner.
10. Restart your Surface and log in with the Kiosk account.

These technological tools and settings allow you to set up a secure, uniform user experience for patrons using your tablets to search and access resources or provide information.

Choosing What to Display to Provide Information Using Mounted Tablets

Your knowledge of your library's space, and the browsing and technology use patterns of your patron base, will be, by far, the best guide for where to mount the tablets in your library and what resources to display on them. Knowing your resources and your audience will spark specific ideas. Here are a few suggestions to get you started, including populations and sections in the library.

- Use mounted tablets to showcase apps recently demonstrated at an Appvisory.
- Display your library's catalog website or app for easy on-the-spot search near the shelves.
- Set up a tablet display of a specific genre of e-books on or near the shelf for print books of the same genre.
- If you're phasing out print magazines and replacing them with digital, use the display space that formerly housed new magazines to showcase tablets loaded with Zinio and other reading apps.

And of course, remember, any decisions you make about how to configure your tablets can be revised, replaced, or otherwise changed as you run the project.

Setting Up Tablets to Gather Patron Data

In addition to setting up tablets to provide information to browsing patrons, you can configure tablets to record patron data, in the form of use patterns. Many of the apps and websites that can be run on your mounted tablets have some means of gathering usage statistics, whether in terms of loading stats on a website, or recording clicks on all, or part of an app. This information can be added to your library's other use and browsing statistics to form a more complete picture of patron behavior.

Using mounted tablets to record patron data in a more personalized way is also easy, thanks to free survey creation websites. You may already have used sites like Google Forms (http://www.google.com/forms/) or SurveyMonkey (http://www.surveymonkey.com) in other library projects, constructing patron surveys and distributing them by e-mail or on social media. Using the kiosk settings described above, you can configure a mounted tablet to display a short patron survey about a topic like library programming, e-book preferences, or even genre reading habits. As with any survey, make sure the data collected is anonymous. Limit the number of demographic questions. Use both cues in the survey and signage near the dedicated kiosk tablet to remind patrons to submit or reset the survey to preserve their privacy.

Running your Mounted Tablet Project

Once your tablets and their mounting hardware have been selected, placed, and configured, what remains is to stay engaged in monitoring their upkeep and use patterns. As with many of the tablet projects outlined throughout this book, the attraction of novelty will mean that patrons are drawn to the tablets almost as soon as they are mounted and activated in the library. As you install and configure the mounted tablets, be sure to test to make sure the configuration presents an intuitive use experience and gives patrons what they need. Use signage near the kiosks requesting feedback, either providing e-mail contact or directing them to the desk to fill out a form. Make sure that staff members are physically keeping an eye on the tablet kiosks and are trained and available to answer questions and elicit feedback. Patrons will be candid, especially about any frustrations they have with the new tablet capabilities!

Checking on the tablet kiosks periodically during library hours is also crucial to maintain their hygiene, especially on days when they see heavy traffic. Maintain physical hygiene with a set of disinfectant wipes or sprays. And give the tablets a quick glance at intervals to make sure that no patron inputs have been inadvertently left on display, resetting the tablets and deleting input if necessary. Because younger patron populations can be even harder on tablets, periodic physical checks of the tablets and accessories for condition and security become especially necessary in children's areas.

After the initial novelty and curiosity about the mounted tablets ebbs over time, there are a few different strategies you can use to renew interest. For tablets displaying suites of apps or selections of e-books, keep them updated by rotating in new titles or app selections tied to more recent Appvisory programs. Encourage and train staff members to guide patrons to tablet kiosks when a reference question merits their use, or to prompt a browsing patron to search using a catalog kiosk. Interest in wall-mounted tablets can be renewed by creating a presentation slideshow of new title images, app icons, or photos of recent library events.

USING YOUR TABLET PROJECTS TO PUBLICIZE THE LIBRARY

A number of the projects outlined here have ended with the section "Taking the Project Further," to help spark ideas for adapting and innovating the project, along with tips and avenues for building publicity and generating interest, such as using social media. No matter what project you choose to start in your own library, you're likely to find that its novelty and visibility means the program basically publicizes itself as soon as you get started, as a number of the librarians interviewed for the library examples in chapter 4 observed. Patrons will be curious about the tablets that they see your staff and other patrons using in the library, or their interest will be piqued by catching a live demonstration. However, make sure that you don't rely entirely on the novelty of the program to generate buzz. Use signage and (secured) displays of the tablets themselves to generate interest. Have librarians incorporate publicizing the tablet program into their outreach and advisory activities, even if their work does not use the tablets directly. Partner with volunteers and power-user patrons to generate buzz for a pilot program, by having active bloggers test the tablets and "live blog" their experience of using them in the library.

By building on and enhancing existing library programs and offering increased opportunities for access and education, your tablet projects work to publicize the library's resources as well. Visible and active tablet programs work to promote the library as a tech-savvy, valuable resource for current information and advice. A broadly trained staff, knowledgeable about a number of devices and apps, is able to deliver more informative and more welcoming service to library patrons. Tablets incorporated into live demonstrations attract and educate patrons and build buzz for the library and its programs. Tablets circulating in your town, emblazoned with the library logo, build word-of-mouth interest. Mounted tablets in your library with eye-catching displays invite exploration of the library's circulating tablets, apps, and other digital media.

No matter the size of your library or the demographics and needs of your patron population, implementing a project such as the ones outlined here showcases the value of your library and its resources. The work, staff time, and equipment that go into planning and running your tablet programs will be a sound investment in the library's mission to equalize digital access and foster an environment for enjoyment and ongoing learning.

6

TIPS AND TRICKS

No matter how you decide to use tablets in your library, or the number and model you choose, some basic guidelines are important to keep in mind. Whether you're in the planning stages of a brand-new tablet program for your library, or looking for a fast answer to improve your existing tablet program, the tips, tricks, and miniprojects in the next few pages are intended as a quick reference, broken down into topics along similar lines to the ideas covered in more detail elsewhere in the book. Use these tips to help you manage the details that go into starting a tablet program and keeping it running smoothly, or to spark innovative ideas for new projects and ways to use tablets in your library. For tips to spark new ideas and take your tablet program further, turn to the very end of this chapter.

PLANNING AND LAUNCHING YOUR TABLET PROGRAM

Reach Out to Colleagues. Reach out to schools and libraries, locally, and across the web and social media, to see what model programs are doing and how you can adapt (or take a look at chapter 4 or Recommended Reading to help you get started.)

Try It Out! Make sure you or your staff get hands-on experience with any hardware, device, or app you're considering for the library. But, even more important than trying demos at stores, trade shows, or other libraries, try to get experience on your own or a borrowed tablet that stretches over a few days (Capdarest-Arest 2015).

Be Open to Inspiration. From a sturdy stand in a dentist's office (S.-A. Taylor 2014a), to app recommendations from a savvy patron, you never know when inspiration or ideas for your program will strike.

Start Small! Even if you already have the plans, and the potential funding, to roll out numerous tablets across your whole system, focusing on small pilot programs will help you manage training, expectations, and workflows (Capdarest-Arest 2015; King 2015).

Planning and Policy. Work across departments to make sure you have policies in place to document

- Borrower eligibility and terms of borrowing
- Responsibility and specific steps to take to restore devices
- How and how often to update backups of user profiles
- App and e-resource collection development including weeding

Learn about Multiple Devices and Apps. Even if your library is offering one or two device platforms, patrons will seek you out for buying advice, app recommendations, even tech support. Keep learning to stay ahead of the curve and be a great resource (Pickup-McMullin 2015).

Test It on Your Target Audience. This is especially important when you're planning a program for younger children. Make sure that the tablets, apps, functions, and stands are responsive to little fingers still working on motor control. Work with younger kids to test tablet mounts as well, to make sure that tablets can securely withstand being pulled and tugged, turned forty-five degrees or more, and that no sharp edges can hurt patrons or fray cords (S.-A. Taylor 2014a).

Ask Your Patrons. Not only will patron surveys help you plan the program, but drawing on patron expertise can help make app selections. And patrons make great volunteers to help teach and demonstrate (Pickup-McMullin 2015).

Take Your Time. Even if you're eager to launch a dazzling new technology program, taking the extra time to research, coordinate, and plan is always valuable, to make sure infrastructures and any necessary partnerships are in place to support it.

Keep Track of Master Account Information. In addition to the master account login and password, you may need to provide your institution name when updating. Keep this information accessible to staff (S.-A. Taylor 2014a).

Master Computer for Backups. Designate one tablet and/or a central desktop computer as the purchasing device to manage app licenses (S.-A. Taylor 2015) and reset the user profile.

Turn Your Library Website into an App. Using screenshots to set up a shortcut of your library's website, you can make a mobile icon that's as accessible as an app on your library tablets (Kraft 2013b).

For iOS:

- Go to the page you want to make into an "app," and tap on the square icon with an arrow at the bottom of the screen.
- Tap "Add to home screen."
- Name it something short and descriptive like "NAME Library."

For Android:

- Bookmark the page.
- Go into Bookmarks menu.
- Click and hold on the bookmark.
- Choose "Add Shortcut to Home."

Budgeting and Financing

Prepaid Cards. Because app stores require a credit card number to be on file with the purchasing account, you may want to use an iTunes gift card or prepaid credit card to purchase apps (King 2015).

Use Existing Library Content and Licenses. They capitalize on your content and they're already paid for (Watson 2015).

Children's Programs

Test Apps. This bears repeating. Especially make sure that the progression between levels makes sense and that there are no surprise hidden fees.

Encourage Collaboration. Even for solo games and unstructured use of tablets in the library, encourage kids to explore apps together.

Use a Timer. For hands-on tablet programs with kids, use a physical timer separate from the tablet to allot device time because the game being played may interfere with the timer sound (S.-A. Taylor 2015).

Test Transitions. Take the time to work through the steps and progressions of an app or educational game, to make sure the jumps in skill level make sense (Mautone 2015), and that there aren't any hidden fees in an otherwise free app (Driscoll, Hurtado, and Rojo 2014).

Learn from Educators. Look for new apps and activity ideas from teachers and schools, as well as educational websites, magazines, and blogs, not just those focused on the library landscape.

Maintaining Devices

Cords, Chargers, and Accessories. Buy extras. Budget to replace lost or damaged cords at least twice a year; and purchase OEM cables, not cheap alternatives (Farid 2015).

Label Everything, Permanently. If possible, etch your library's name and the item barcode into the device itself, as well as labeling any cases and cords. If your cataloging setup allows it, create barcodes and separate catalog entries for each item being loaned out.

Security Settings. No matter your operating system, management safeguards, or other features you have in place, users will circumvent them. In addition to your usual process of restoring settings (whether wiping completely or to a default profile), take the time to double check that there's nothing extra added (King 2015).

Set Up a Code to Delete Apps. Work with IT to set up a permission code to delete apps, to prevent patrons from deleting apps. This can be configured in tablets' settings (Kraft 2015).

Restoring Settings (iPad). Using the Restore from Backup function through iTunes without restoring the device to factory settings will *not* erase user content from a device. Instead, wipe the iPad to factory settings, then restore loaded apps and books from the Master Backup. And remember to update the Master Backup on a regular basis (Small 2015).

Passcode Problems (iPads). Libraries of all types and sizes have reported issues with iPads and passcode problems. The current configuration allows patrons to take control of borrowed iPads using the Find My iPad feature, meaning that a patron can take full ownership of a device, locking it to the patron's own credentials (Farid 2015). If a patron sets up a passcode or activation lock on a borrowed device, that patron may need to be contacted to disable it before patron data can be wiped and reset (Woodbury 2015). While one fix for the issue is to connect the device to the master updating computer, resetting an iPad a patron has reconfigured remains a headache (S.-A. Taylor 2014b).

Repair and Warranty (iPads). Remember that Apple will not renew AppleCare contracts after the first three years, so any damage to the iPads' cords, body, or screen will need to be repaired at the library's expense (Farid 2015).

Weed Your Apps and Devices, Too. Just like print and other media, devices and apps can get old and obsolete, or show wear and tear. Make time to assess and pull devices that are worn and delete apps that are obsolete or unused.

Programs in Your Library

Practice Navigating Apps in a Mirror before Demos. When you're doing a program that uses a projection screen, make sure to allow extra time to practice with the projector . . . or try using a mirror to get the same perspective.(Driscoll, Hurtado, and Rojo 2014).

Enhance Library Displays. Add an interactive element to shelf-talkers and other static visual displays in your library by adding QR codes you or your patrons can use to access enhanced information. Or use an augmented reality app like Layar Reality Browser for iOS or Augment or Aurasma for Android.

Code and Create. There are a lot of great apps and programs to help teach code at all ages. Or you can invite coding and tinkering with app-driven devices like OzoBot for kids (Roalsen 2015).

Continued Learning

Browse Social Media. The list of articles and blogs in Recommended Reading will be a good start to your further reading, but reading a wide range of education and tech blogs, in addition to library blogs, is a great idea. Librarians on Twitter, Facebook, and Tumblr can be a great resource as well, whether posting links to interesting articles or sharing their own insights in bite-size status updates.

Stay Connected with Conferences. Whether attending a conference in person or following its hashtags on social media, conferences can be a terrific resource for developing new ideas.

Especially watch for

- Presentations on case studies and libraries' pilot tablet programs.
- Appvisory presentations, whether general or focused on a specific topic or group.
- Demonstrations of peripheral devices and gadgets that can connect with tablets.
- Topics around makerspaces, hacking, or coding.
- "60 Apps in 60 Minutes" presentations. (Make sure you get the slides for these afterward! Keeping track while you're attending can be difficult.)

7

FUTURE TRENDS

During the final stages of writing this book, Apple announced the release of a new MacBook, with a sleeker design, and the advent of the AppleWatch, the latest in wearable technology. This might leave busy librarians wondering how they and their library programs can keep up with what's happening now, much less plan for or even wonder about what the next big thing might be.

There's no question that staying connected and staying mobile will be important to our patrons, and that tablets will continue the trend of becoming more powerful and more affordable, possibly following the path of the cell phone in becoming a commodity (Rainie 2015). "Although it's a little bit hard to foresee the future of tablets as we now understand the gadget, it's safe to say that more and more people will be reading and browsing on digital devices," says Lee Rainie, whether on laptops or tablets, or with the new mid-size "phablets" at a size between cell phones and tablets. According to Rainie, who is director of Internet, Science and Technology Research at Pew Research Center, while it is unclear as yet how device adoptions and preference will play out, a generational divide between younger users reading on smaller screens while older readers gravitate toward tablets could play a role (Rainie 2015). The trend toward being able to interact with a device through gesture, voice, or other mode of command speaks to changes in the use patterns and perhaps the overall importance of tablets, which have historically had the competitive advantage of easy typing to key information into a touch screen interface. It may be, Rainie adds, that the type of device matters less than the interplay between them, as people choose between increasingly connected devices, sharing the data of daily life across the Internet of Things.

"Importantly, communications networks will also improve, offering ever greater speed, enabling not only streaming but also remote use of applications such as photo and video editing," predicts Jeff Jarvis (2015), director of the Tow-Knight Center for Entrepreneurial Journalism and author of *Public Parts: How Sharing in the Digital Age Improves the Way We Work and Live* . He adds that one future option would be for libraries to support patrons accessing their own data and devices, through the cloud, for example, by providing dumb screens as a portal for patron access. However, he acknowledges that this comes with an addition to the library's existing and longstanding responsibility to protect the rights they have always cherished, the protection of privacy around the use of information in tandem with open access and sharing (Jarvis 2015).

No matter the evolution of technology, libraries will still, and always, matter. "The most cutting-edge libraries are already talking about how to adjust to the Internet of Things, to use big data. . . . I really like the notion that the library can think of itself as an all-service, connector institution rather than an endpoint information-dispensing organization," Rainie says. He points to exciting conversations evolving about the role of libraries as a transcending "third place," extending their role as a platform for access and for fostering connections within the community (Aspen Institute, Dialog on Public Libraries 2014). The ability to access and work with information in new ways, whether through tablets, technology, or facilitating library programs, is more about the role libraries and librarians play, using the tools at hand to deliver what their patrons need and want.

Jarvis also sees impressive potential for starting with patron needs, to reimagine what a library can be. "I see people hacking libraries to become new workspaces, new meeting spaces, new makerspaces. I see industries from journalism to technology using the skills of a librarian to gather, analyze, and visualize data" (Jarvis 2015). Taking it a step further, he invites "librarians to imagine their work without buildings and even books. What is their value then? How can they bring value to people using the tools the net brings?"

Confronting that question and the larger question about the role of libraries in the information landscape can feel overwhelming, especially here, at the end of a book walking through the myriad possibilities and options of integrating tablet devices into your library program.

Once again, it is useful to step back and remember what we, as librarians, have always known.

Bonnie Roalsen, youth services librarian at the Dover Town Library sums it up beautifully: "As we continue to integrate more social or learning objects into our collections, we are providing better service and experiential learning opportunities to a much broader scope of users than we previously could. Now we can address the needs of all different types of learners with all different types of learning styles effectively, and help them engage with topics and knowledge as we never could before."

No matter the size, platform, or apps you choose for your tablet programs, the end goal is always the same: bringing your patrons a richer information experience.

RECOMMENDED READING

PRINT RESOURCES

Aspen Institute, Dialog on Public Libraries. 2014. *Rising to the Challenge: Re-Envisioning Public Libraries*. White paper. Aspen, CO: The Aspen Institute. Also available at http://csreports.aspeninstitute.org/documents//AspenLibrariesReport.pdf. Read for ideas and inspiration about libraries' role in the changing information landscape and keep an eye on future reports.

Capdarest-Arest, Nicole. 2013. "Implementing a Tablet Circulation Program on a Shoestring." *Journal of the Medical Library Association* (July 10, 2013): 220–24. Good guide to implementing a tablet program for any busy academic library setting.

Hahn, Jim. 2013. *The Best 100 Free Apps for Libraries*. Lanham, MD: The Scarecrow Press. Well-organized guide to apps to improve library services, with use cases for Utility Apps, Augmented Reality Apps, Productivity Apps, and Social Apps.

Hennig, Nicole. 2014. *Selecting and Evaluating the Best Mobile Apps for Library Services*. Chicago: ALA TechSource. Systematic guide to evaluating apps for library use. For updates, see Hennig's blog at http://nicolehennig.com/.

BLOGS AND WEBSITES

Code4Lib. http://code4lib.org/ Information professionals, technologists, designers, architects, and curators exchange and develop ideas about using technology in cultural spaces.

David Lee King: Social Web, Emerging Trends, and Libraries. www.davidleeking.com/. Discusses emerging tech, user behavior, and strategies for libraries.

Krafty Librarian. www.kraftylibrarian.com/. Medical librarian Michelle Kraft blogs about technology use in libraries as well as issues related to medical librarianship.

Lynda.com. http://www.lynda.com/. Subscription database with tutorials on coding, design, and business.

OCLC WebJunction Library Stories. http://www.webjunction.org/ share-your-story/news.html. Includes some great case studies about starting and running tablet and technology programs in libraries. Two articles by Sally-Adrina Taylor of Rapid City Public Libraries deserve special mention:"iFought the iPads (and iWon)," *OCLC WebJunction* (March 28, 2014), http://www.webjunction.org/news/webjunction/ ifought-the-ipads-and-iwon.html; "You Shall Not Pass! iPad Passcode Programs and Other Insights," *OCLC WebJunction* (August 11, 2014), http://www.webjunction.org/news/webjunction/you-shall-not-pass-ipad-passcode-problems-and-other-insights.html.

The Digital Shift. http://www.thedigitalshift.com/. Focuses on new media in libraries.

TechSoup for Libraries. http://www.techsoup.org/libraries. Advice on selecting hardware and software, funding tech programs, and Cookbooks—guides on running and maintaining tech programs.

REFERENCES

Abdullah-Abouelaziz, Cheryl. 2015. Interview by Elizabeth Willse. Director, Dover Town Library (February 27, 2015).

American Academy of Pediatrics Council on Communications and Media. 2011. *Media Use by Children Younger Than 2 Years.* Policy statement. Elk Grove, IL: American Academy of Pediatrics.

Annoyed Librarian. 2014. "The Library as Third Place." *Library Journal,* February 17. http://lj.libraryjournal.com/blogs/annoyedlibrarian/2014/02/17/the-library-as-third-place/ (accessed March 6, 2015).

Apple. 2015. *iOS: About Guided Access.* February 5. https://support.apple.com/en-us/HT202612 (accessed April 6, 2015).

Aspen Institute, Dialog on Public Libraries. 2014. *Rising to the Challenge: Re-Envisioning Public Libraries.* White paper. Aspen, CO: The Aspen Institute.

Berger, J. 2012. "Queens Libraries Speak the Mother Tongue." *New York Times,* January 2.

Bonner, Scott, interview by Elizabeth Willse. Director of the Ferguson Public Library (March 3, 2015).

Campbell, C. 2014. "Children's Librarians as Digital Media Mentors." Fred Rogers Center for Early Learning and Children's Media at St. Vincent's College. April 14. http://www.fredrogerscenter.org/blog/childrens-librarians-as-digital-media-mentors.

Capdarest-Arest, Nicole. 2013. "Implementing a Tablet Circulation Program on a Shoestring." *Journal of the Medical Library Association,* July 10, 220–24.

———. 2015. Interview by Elizabeth Willse. Emerging Technologies Librarian at University of Arizona College of Medicine (March 2, 2015).

Driscoll, Jennifer, Annmarie Hurtado, and Zyrel Rojo. 2014. "'Appvisory' in the Children's Library." Presentation. Pasadena, California, October 2.

Epps, Lisa, and Kelvin Watson. 2014. "2014 Library of the Future Award: Emergency! How Queens Library Came to Patrons' Rescue After Hurricane Sandy." *Computers in Libraries,* December, 3–5, 30.

Farid, Farrukh. 2015. Interview by Elizabeth Willse. Manager of IT at Dr. Martin Luther King Jr. Library, San Jose State University (March 5, 2015).

Flood, A. 2014. "Bookless Library Opened by New US University." *The Guardian,* August 29. http://www.theguardian.com/books/2014/aug/29/bookless-library-new-us-university-florida-polytechnic-digital (accessed March 2, 2015).

Hanel, Trevor. 2015. Interview by Elizabeth Willse. Reference Librarian, Cedar Rapids Public Library (February 25, 2015).

IDC Worldwide. 2014. "Fueled by Back-to-School Promotions and US Growth, the Global Tablet Market Grows 11% in the Third Quarter According to IDC." *IDC Tracker,* October. http://www.idc.com/getdoc.jsp?containerId=prUS25225114 (accessed March 6, 2015).

———. 2015. "Global Market Share Held by Tablet Vendors from 2nd Quarter 2011 to 4th Quarter 2014." *Statista.* http://www.statista.com/statistics/276635/market-share-held-by-tablet-vendors/ (accessed March 6, 2015).

Jarvis, Jeff. 2015. Interview by Elizabeth Willse. Director of the Tow-Knight Center for Entrepreneurial Journalism (March 9, 2015).

King, David Lee. 2015. Interview by Elizabeth Willse. Digital Services Director at Topeka & Shawnee County Public Library (February 24, 2015).

Kraft, Michelle. 2013a. "iPad's Use and Value Is Related to Hospital's Infrastructure." *Krafty Librarian,* November 19. http://www.kraftylibrarian.com/ipad-use-value-is-related-to-hospitals-infrastructure/ (accessed March 4, 2015).

———. 2013b. "Quick & Dirty Way to Make a Library App." *Krafty Librarian.* September 25, 2013. http://www.kraftylibrarian.com/quick-dirty-way-to-make-a-library-app/ (accessed March 8, 2015).

———. 2015. Interview by Elizabeth Willse. Senior Medical Librarian at Cleveland Clinic Medical Library (March 7, 2015).

Leadbetter, Jared. 2015. Interview by Elizabeth Willse. Technology Coordinator at Maine State Library (February 6, 2015).

Lerner, C. and R. Barr. 2013. *Screen Sense: Setting the Record Straight Research-Based Guidelines for Screen Use for Children Under 3 Years Old.* Washington, DC: National Center for Infants, Toddlers, Children and Families.

Mautone, Mark. 2015. Interview by Elizabeth Willse. Lead teacher, Autism/ABA, Hoboken Public School District (February 26, 2015).

McFarland, Matt. 2014. "Libraries without Books Find a Niche in San Antonio." *Washington Post Innovations Blog,* December 16. http://www.washingtonpost.com/blogs/innovations/wp/2014/12/16/libraries-without-physical-books-find-a-niche-in-san-antonio/ (accessed March 2015).

Miller, Laura. 2015. Interview by Elizabeth Willse. Circulation Manager at L.E. Phillips Memorial Library (February 16, 2015).

Moore, Claire. 2015. Interview by Elizabeth Willse. Head of Children's Services at Darien Library (February 9, 2015).

NCSU Libraries. 2014. "Suma." *NCSU Libraries,* July 25. http://www.lib.ncsu.edu/reports/suma (accessed March 9, 2015).

Pickup-McMullin, Kate. 2015. Interview by Elizabeth Willse. Tech Ninja and Assistant Director at the Southwest Harbor Public Library (March 1, 2015).

Pollakoff, Stan. 2015. Interview by Elizabeth Willse. Library Director at Sussex Library (February 2015).

Rainie, Lee. 2015. Interview by Elizabeth Willse. Director of Internet, Science and Technology Research at Pew Research Center (March 9, 2015).

Rathbone, Andy. 2014. *Surface for Dummies.* Hoboken, NJ: John Wiley & Sons.

Roalsen, Bonnie. 2015. Interview by Elizabeth Willse. Head of Youth Services, Dover Town Library (March 11, 2015).

Small, Isa. 2015. Interview by Elizabeth Willse. Programming and Communication Service Manager, L.E. Phillips Memorial Library (February 27, 2015).

Steele, Chandra. 2013. "History of the iPad." *PCMAG.com,* October 22. http://www.pcmag.com/slideshow/story/295265/history-of-the-ipad (accessed March 6, 2015).

Strasburger, V. C., M. J. Hogan, D. A. Mulligan, N. Ameenuddin, D. A. Christakis, C. Cross, and W. S. L. Swanson. 2013. "Children, Adolescents, and the Media." *Pediatrics*: October 23, 2013, 958–61. http://pediatrics.aapiblications.org/content/132/5/958.full.

Sun, C. 2014. "Appvisory for Educational Children's Apps, TDS14." *The Digital Shift,* October 3. http://www.thedigitalshift.com/2014/10/k-12/appvisory-educational-apps-tds14/.

Taylor, Sally-Adrina. 2014a. "iFought the iPads (and iWon)." *WebJunction,* March 28. http://www.webjunction.org/news/webjunction/ifought-the-ipads-and-iwon.html (accessed February 24, 2015).

————. 2014b. "You Shall Not Pass! iPad Passcode Problems and Other Insights." *WebJunction,* August 11. http://www.webjunction.org/news/webjunction/you-shall-not-pass-ipad-passcode-problems-and-other-insights.html (accessed February 24, 2015).

————. 2015. Interview by Elizabeth Willse. Associate in Public Services for Rapid City Public Libraries (February 26, 2015).

Taylor, Stacy. 2015. Interview by Elizabeth Willse. Emerging Technologies Librarian at Nielsen Library, Adams State University (February 26, 2015).

Watson, Kelvin. 2015. Interview by Elizabeth Willse. Vice President Digital Services & Strategy and General Manager at Queens Library Enterprises (March 2, 2015).

Woodbury, David. 2015. Interview by Elizabeth Willse. Associate Head of User Experience, North Carolina State University at Raleigh (February 25, 2015).

Zickuhr, Kathryn, Kristen Purcell, and Lee Rainie. 2014. *Library Engagement Typology.* White paper. Washington, DC: Pew Research Center. March.

Zickuhr, Kathryn, and Lee Rainie. 2014. *E-Reading Rises as Device Ownership Jumps.* White paper. Washington, DC: Pew Research Center. January.

INDEX

ABOUT THE AUTHOR

Elizabeth Willse received her master's in library and information science from Pratt Institute. Her key area of study has been an examination of how library practice is evolving at the intersection of traditional and digital media, seeking ways to harness both to improve outreach and instruction. A freelance writer with over a decade of experience, her writing has appeared in publications such as the *Newark Star-Ledger*, *Women's Health Magazine*, *ChelseaNow*, and numerous web outlets. She currently works as a librarian at Berkeley College in New York.

NORTH COUNTRY LIBRARY SYSTEM

0 11 01 0353282 3

MAR - - 2016